ADVANCE PRAISE FOR

Black Women's Activism

"It is both useful and pleasing that Rita B. Dandridge's study of historical romances honors a long-standing tradition in American literature of respecting literature that combines *utile* and *dulce*. She combines factual contexts with accessible readings of text that too many intellectuals have too quickly dismissed as mere recreational reading. The result is that we joyfully learn more about some of today's best-selling and most popular African American writers while we come to appreciate more clearly their innovative and radical interventions regarding race, class, and gender stereotypes of our past and of our present."

Frances Smith Foster, Charles Howard Candler Professor of English and Women's Studies, Emory University

"This text is a thoughtful, scholarly, and valuable genre study that addresses the neglect of black women's historical romances and the black activist's role in this genre. Rita B. Dandridge's study offers new insights and exciting alternative perspectives to scholars and students of African-American women's literature."

Freddy L. Thomas, Chair, Department of Languages and Literature, Virginia State University

I0879824

Black Women's Activism

AFRICAN AMERICAN LITERATURE AND CULTURE

Expanding and Exploding the Boundaries

Carlyle V. Thompson
General Editor

Vol. 5

PETER LANG
New York • Washington, D.C./Baltimore • Bern
Frankfurt am Main • Berlin • Brussels • Vienna • Oxford

Rita B. Dandridge

Black Women's Activism

Reading African American Women's Historical Romances

PETER LANG
New York • Washington, D.C./Baltimore • Bern
Frankfurt am Main • Berlin • Brussels • Vienna • Oxford

Library of Congress Cataloging-in-Publication Data

Dandridge, Rita B.
Black women's activism : reading African American women's historical romances / Rita B. Dandridge.
p. cm. — (African-American literature and culture; v. 5)
Includes bibliographical references and index.
1. American fiction—African American authors—History and criticism. 2. Literature and history—United States—History—20th century. 3. Literature and society—United States—History—20th century. 4. American fiction—Women authors—History and criticism. 5. Historical fiction, American—History and criticism. 6. African American women—Intellectual life. 7. African American women in literature. 8. African Americans in literature. 9. Social problems in literature. 10. Social action in literature. I. Title. II. Series.
PS374.N4 D36 813.009'9287'08996073—dc21 2002156547
ISBN 0-8204-6734-0
ISSN 1528-3887

Bibliographic information published by **Die Deutsche Bibliothek**. **Die Deutsche Bibliothek** lists this publication in the "Deutsche Nationalbibliografie"; detailed bibliographic data is available on the Internet at http://dnb.ddb.de/.

Cover design by Lisa Barfield

275 Seventh Avenue, 28th Floor, New York, NY 10001
www.peterlangusa.com

Contents

Acknowledgments

I began work on this project soon after I attended a Umoja Festival in downtown Portsmouth, Virginia, in the fall of 1997. It was at that festival that Anita Richmond Bunkley's *Black Gold* caught my eye. A collector of African American women's novels, I grabbed the last copy and handed the tent keeper a ten-dollar bill.

Three months passed before I found the time to read *Black Gold;* during the winter break when the demands of university teaching and the urgency of domesticity eased, I found the saga of Leela Wilder, an oil field owner, a page-turner. The enthusiasm I experienced in reading this historical romance and others published in the 1990s was soon challenged when I attempted to locate critical commentaries about them. The present project grew out of a need to introduce a group of recent narratives that I feel have as much validity as more well-known, critically examined works.

For making this project possible, I extend acknowledgments to colleagues and friends.

I thank Shirley R. Steinberg and her husband Joe L. Kincheloe, who suggested this project for Peter Lang Publishing at its "Getting Your Work Published" Workshop, held at Norfolk State University in spring 2002.

Thanks go to Gwendolyn E. Osborne, reviewer for *Romance Reader,* who facilitated my contacts with the writers and bought and sent me a copy of Gay G. Gunn's *Nowhere to Run*. Thanks, Gwen, for introducing me to a writer I did not know existed.

My gratitude extends to colleagues who took the time from their busy schedules to read various chapters of this manuscript and offer critical suggestions: Hortense E. Simmons, University of California, Sacramento; Frances Foster Smith, Emory University; Joe L. Kincheloe, City University of New York; SallyAnn Ferguson, University of North Carolina, Greensboro; and Freddy L. Thomas, Virginia State University.

I thank Marietta Weary Scott and Carole Martin, who offered encouragement and provided valuable information for chapter 1 on Mary Ellen Pleasant and California history.

I extend thanks also to Norfolk State University librarians Mable G. Butts, Velma Haley, Cynthia L. Harrison, and Manju Majumdar, who offered untiring assistance in securing information through interlibrary loan and various databases for this project.

Thanks go also to Damani J. Drew for his advice and technical support.

Gay G. Gunn. *Nowhere to Run*. Columbus, OH: Genesis Press, copyright © 1997. All rights reserved.

Darlene Clark Hine and Kathleen Thompson, eds. *A Shining Thread of Hope: The History of Black Women in America*. New York: Broadway Books, copyright © 1998. Reprinted by permission of publisher. All rights reserved.

Belinda Hurmence, ed. *Before Freedom: 48 Oral Histories of Former North and South Carolina Slaves*. Winston-Salem: John F. Blair, Publisher, copyright © 1990. Reprinted by permission of publisher. All rights reserved.

Teresa de Lauretis. *Technologies of Gender: Essays on Theory, Film, and Fiction*. Bloomington: Indiana University Press, copyright © 1987. Reprinted by permission of publisher. All rights reserved.

Teresa de Lauretis. *Technologies of Gender: Essays on Theory, Film, and Fiction*. London: Palgrave Macmillan, copyright © 1987. Reproduced by permission of publisher. All rights reserved.

Elmer P. Martin and Joanne Mitchell Martin. *Social Work and the Black Experience*. Washington D.C.: National Association of Social Workers, Inc., Copyright © 1995. Reprinted by permission of publisher. All rights reserved.

Thomas Szasz. *The Manufacture of Madness: A Comparative Study of the Inquisition and the Mental Health Movement*. Syracuse: Syracuse University Press, copyright © 1997. All rights reserved.

Mary Roth Walsh. *"Doctors Wanted: No Women Need Apply": Sexual Barriers in the Medical Profession, 1835–1975*. New Haven: Yale University Press, copyright © 1977. All rights reserved.

Wilbur H. Watson. *Black Folk Medicine*. Piscataway, NJ: Transaction Publishers, copyright © 1984. Reprinted by permission of publisher. All rights reserved.

Patricia Yaeger. *Honey-Mad Women: Emancipatory Strategies in Women's Writing*. New York: Columbia University Press, copyright © 1988. Reprinted by permission of publisher. All rights reserved.

Introduction

Reading African American Women's Historical Romances

This study explores black women's activism in African American women's popular historical romances that debuted in 1989 with Anita Richmond Bunkley's *Emily, the Yellow Rose*. Considered the "second wave" of historical romances, Bunkley's *Emily* and the post-1989 narratives that followed it situate the black female protagonist as agent of resistance in the nineteenth and early twentieth centuries. Following the black militant and black feminist movements, these narratives expand the nature of black female characters found in earlier historical romances by offering a fuller view of them as they struggle at the forefront of specific historic moments.

Black women's second wave of historical romances re-create the black woman in the nineteenth century, a dynamic period in which black women made invigorating calls to action and empowerment. As early as 1832, Maria Stewart, considered to be the first black womanist, made a call for black women's action.[1] In "An Address Delivered before the Afric-American Female Intelligence Society of America," Stewart argued, "It is useless for us any longer to sit with our hands folded, reproaching the whites; for that will never elevate us. Possess the spirit of independence. . . . Possess the spirit of men, bold and enterprising, fearless and undaunted."[2] This message encapsulates a crucial issue for black women in the nineteenth century: The qualities perceived as necessary for significant change in relations between the races and sexes are gendered male. Stewart's call to action and plea for independence resonated throughout the nineteenth and early twentieth centuries as black women began to assume public positions as abolitionists (Harriet Tubman), teachers (Anna Julia Cooper), doctors (Rebecca Lee), and journalists (Mary Shadd Cary).

This book was conceived in response to the overwhelming neglect that late-twentieth-century black women's historical romances have garnered in popular and contemporary literary studies and to critics' subsequent failure to interpret the black female activist's role in this genre. Critics have cited various reasons for neglecting historical romances. George Dekker says the content is "swollen with specimens deformed by . . . racism [and] sexism,"[3] Nikki Giovanni believes romantic interludes are boring and destructive,[4] and M. Giulia Fabi argues that males are disinterested in women's fiction.[5] These divergent reasons for neglecting black women's historical romances are excuses some critics make for rejecting works outside the canon. Glenwood Irons puts it boldly when he says, "The arbitrary division between great literature and popular narratives has over time been ruthlessly exposed. Critics have come to set the division as an artificial construct that has little to do with quality and much to do with changeable notions of canonicity."[6] Despite the artificial constructs that critics have erected against black women's historical romances, the fact remains that how one reads these narratives determines their relevance to and expansion of African American women's literature and the historical romance genre. To set forth a critical interpretation of African American women's twentieth-century historical romances and black women's struggles to actualize self, I offer four arguments for reading these narratives: 1) They have literary value, 2) They have political importance, 3) They illuminate a womanist narratology, and 4) They engage an African-centered helping tradition. In this study, these arguments will be analyzed in the narratives of five authors: Anita Richmond Bunkley,[7] Beverly Jenkins,[8] Shirley Hailstock,[9] Francine Craft,[10] and Gay G. Gunn.[11]

Before a discussion of the four arguments begins, a brief look at early African American historical romances and their relation to the wider genre is necessary for orientation.

The First Wave of Historical Romances

The historical romance is one of the oldest literary forms in African American literature, having evolved through such minor works as William Wells Brown's drama *The Escape; or, A Leap for Freedom* (1858) and Frances Harper's short story "The Two Offers" (1859). William Wells Brown's *Clotel; or, the President's Daughter* (1853) is the earliest known historical romance written by an African

American. African American women's historical romance novels, the focus of this study, can be traced to Frances Harper's *Minnie's Sacrifice* (1869), a serialized novel first published in *The Christian Recorder*. This was followed by Harper's *Sowing and Reaping* (1876–77), *Trial and Triumph* (1888–89), and *Iola Leroy, or Shadows Uplifted* (1892). Twentieth-century historical romances include, but are not limited to, Pauline Hopkins's *Contending Forces: A Romance Illustrative of Negro Life North and South* (1900), Zora Neale Hurston's *Their Eyes Were Watching God* (1937), Margaret Walker's *Jubilee* (1966), Toni Morrison's *Beloved* (1987), and Gloria Naylor's *Mama Day* (1988). These early historical romances had as their primary function to address the sociohistorical issues challenging African Americans as a race at specific historical moments. This specific function coincided with the broader sociopolitical intention of modern historical romances, which called attention to the struggles of various cultures and ethnic groups throughout history. As early pieces, African American writings revise and expand issues and territory presented in historical romances written by nineteenth-century southern white male writers such as William Alexander Caruthers, John Pendleton Kennedy, and Henry Gilmore Simms, who inherited the genre popularized by English writer Sir Walter Scott in his Waverley Novels.

The modern historical romance evolved in the nineteenth century as a sociohistorical genre with a revolutionary impetus. Its centerpiece is the battle or struggle between two opposing political forces over unresolved sociopolitical issues. To state it simply, Sir Walter Scott's Loyalists versus their opponents became Unionists versus Confederates in southern white American literature and black freedom fighters (and their allies) versus oppressive whites in African American literature. The struggles presage humankind's attempts to solve political differences and transform the world into a better place to inhabit. Romance functions as a counterpoint to enmity, a tentative relief from war. It usually occurs between two persons holding similar political ideas, and marriage is often the result. The term *historical romance,* then, refers to a variety of fictional works with a definite historical setting containing political combatants representing the time defined and engaging in adventure and romantic affairs.

Early African American women writers including Frances Harper and Pauline Hopkins found the historical romance a useful and timely genre in which to encase unresolved sociopolitical issues regarding African Americans' rights and status in American society. Characters inveigh against unlawful remanding of free blacks to slavery, political and educational disenfranchisement, and lynching. The revolutionary times that these authors write about—the Civil War and Reconstruction—failed to bring the desired results in the period the authors wrote in. That is to say, full citizenship promised to African

Americans during the course of the Civil War remained an unresolved issue at the turn of the twentieth century. Social reform, therefore, became a primary mission of these early writers.

A New Image in the Genre

African American women writers of historical romances from 1989 to the present have a different mission than their literary predecessors. More than one hundred years removed from the historical period that they write about, these authors have as their primary purpose to plug the sociohistorical gaps left by earlier writers. Through carefully researched history, evident by extensive bibliographies appended to some of their novels, late-twentieth-century black women writers of nineteenth- and early-twentieth-century historical romances offer a fuller view of specific historic moments, an expanded look at black womanhood, a more complex and emphatic involvement of black women in historic settings, and heated romance. Realistic emotions circumscribe these black heroines, who assume an oppositional stance against various sociohistorical issues that affect their race, gender, and class.

My primary argument for reading the second wave of African American women's historical romances is to show how they expand conventions found in earlier African American historical romances that utilized innovations in the genre popularized by Sir Walter Scott. At the outset, the novels under discussion, beginning with Bunkley's *Emily*, extend the paradigm of the African American historical romance, generally considered a masculine genre because either its best-known writers are men—William Brown, W. E. B. Du Bois, Frank Yerby—or because the novels celebrate the victories of men. Even one of Pauline Hopkins's early historical romances, *Of One Blood; or, The Hidden Self* (1902–3), celebrates the exploits of a male protagonist. In contrast, the second wave of historical romances is written by and about African American women. These novels pay tribute to strong nineteenth-century African American women who as a race, gender, and class were considered at the time to have minimal significance in society. The novels celebrate the desires, feats, professions, and relationships of black women, not white men or black men. The literary value of these novels is the new image that black heroines bring to the genre.

The new image is that of the dark-hued heroine who triumphs. This figure revises the mulatta stereotype dominant in early African American historical romances and descended from the tradition of the blond, fair lady populating the traditional genre. In the later works, the dark-skinned heroine is a masculinized or toughened character, whereas her light-complexioned counterpart is too often perceived in black male and female fiction as too weak to effect societal change. In *Clotel*, for instance, William Wells Brown concedes power to white men as Clotel, the mulatta protagonist, drowns herself in the Potomac River when she discovers herself trapped and helpless in the patriarchal institution of slavery. Nearly a century later, Frank Yerby's *The Foxes of Harrow* (1946) explores the adventures of the white Stephen Harrow while minimizing the presence of his Creole mistress. Dispensing with weak, light-complexioned heroines, post-1989 black writers of historical romances give victory to strong black women darker than mulattas. These narratives celebrate black women's victories in the tradition of black women pioneers who paved the freedom path.

African American women's recent historical romances further expand the genre by complicating the male plot structure of adventure and conquest. These novels, in which the African American heroine appears, contain what I refer to as a "maternal thread." They are stitched in a fabric of maternal tropes suggesting a desired insemination, pregnancy, and birth. The heroine activist longs for identity formation as a woman, chooses to create a new life for herself (insemination aided by a vicarious male copula), reacts to the pains and stresses of her productiveness (gestation encrusted in the reality of a warped and flawed social history), and rejoices in birth (self-actualization with the production of seedlings, such as advisees, students, and patients). The maternal paradigm is superimposed on a masculine-like tale of adventure and romance. The texts in which the maternal and masculine threads exist should be read as obstructional discourse. These narratives occlude the abortive adventures in earlier historical romances of heroines who either sublimate their desires or fail to engage themselves in a successful public career. The dual threads that guide these novels allow the women to complete their adventure and to function both as maternal figures and as masculine-like warriors in public careers. How these heroines further expand the portrait of black women in the historical romances will be discerned as my arguments continue.

My second argument for reading these late-twentieth-century narratives is to bring attention to their political importance. While romantic fiction may seem to avoid the political realm entirely, black women's historical romances actually take strong political positions. As Barbara Smith argues in her 1977 groundbreaking essay, "Toward a Black Feminist Criticism," a black woman's "approach to literature that embodies a realization that the politics of sex as well as the politics of race and class are crucially interlocking factors in the works of black women writers is an absolute necessity."[12] Black women's historical romances are factional narratives and should be read for the race/gender/class elements that Smith mentions. In these narratives, issues of race, gender, and class are exposed, politicized, and targeted.

Black women's historical romances document race as a social and political construct that is anchored to a systemic body of laws based on color difference, privileging whites over blacks. These historical romances recount a period in which Thomas Jefferson, cosigner of the Declaration of Independence and third president of the United States, for instance, pondered the question of color difference and acquiesced to laws that separated the races: "Whether the black of the negro resides in the reticular membrane between the skin and scarf-skin, or in the scarf-skin itself; whether it proceeds from the colour of the blood, the colour of the bile, or from that of some other secretion, the difference is . . . real."[13] The reality of color difference, which politicians such as Jefferson acknowledged, meant an inferior identity and existence for blacks generally. An inferior identity and an existence based on color difference made their entry into America during slavery, argues Evelyn Higginbotham, African American womanist-historian.[14] Blacks' inhuman treatment, emanating from color difference during and after slavery, galvanized black women protagonists to action in the historical romances.

In these narratives, black women activists affirm their self-identities in a politically charged, racially segregated environment. They seize the moment to sculpt their reality. Bunkley's *Emily, the Yellow Rose*, for instance, politicizes race in the struggles of Emily Morgan, an antebellum free black woman with second-class status. Migrating to the Mexican colony of Texas to obtain full citizenship, Emily struggles to maintain her free status in that new frontier, where Anglos defy Mexican laws against slavery. Likewise, Beverly Jenkins's *Indigo* (1996) addresses the human rights issue in America's democracy that persisted in establishing racial barriers based on color that had no rational justification. Hester Wyatt, protagonist, abolitionist, and fictional re-creation of Harriet Tubman, risks her life as conductor of the Underground Railroad. Bunkley and Jenkins are extending a literary tradition that Frances Harper and Pauline Hopkins pioneered in their nineteenth-century historical romances.

As early as 1869, in *Minnie's Sacrifice*, Frances Harper recorded the limitations of race that Minnie and Louis experience as mulattoes.[15] Later, in a note appended to *Iola Leroy* (1892), Harper speaks of racism as the "unsolved American problem" and states her novel's purpose: "From threads of fact and fiction I have woven a story whose mission will not be in vain if it awaken in the hearts of our countrymen a stronger sense of justice and a more Christlike humanity in behalf of those whom the fortunes of war threw homeless, ignorant, and poor, upon the threshold of a new era."[16] And less than a decade later, Pauline Hopkins prefaces her novel *Contending Forces* (1900) with the following: "In giving this little romance expression in print, I am not actuated by a desire for notoriety or for profit, but to do all that I can in an humble way to raise the stigma of degradation from my race."[17]

As literary foremothers, Harper and Hopkins protest racism as a deterrent to the heroine's evolving as a whole person, and they create model, mulatta heroines to point to the injustices meted out to the race. Jenkins's Hester Wyatt, on the other hand, is a dark-skinned woman, approximating the dark hue of Harriet Tubman. Her coloring acknowledges the presence of dark-skinned women in the race, and the role they played in uplifting it. Unlike Harper's depiction of Iola Leroy as the beautiful octoroon who is morally upright, "to refute," as Barbara Christian argues, "the popular stereotype of the day that blacks were degenerates," Beverly Jenkins rewrites history as it was.[18] Hester is a more plausible fictional representative than Iola of a black woman who demands the same rights as whites; Iola, created in the image of whites, becomes a distorted "cultural missionary" who seems better than whites. Post-1989 historical romances modify Harper's and Hopkins's images of mulatta heroines to include the darker-hued African American woman. I argue that this image modification offers a more comprehensive representation of the race and allows the darker-hued woman a greater realism and sensitivity to her African culture and heritage than her mulatta counterpart.

Race as a political theme merges with that of gender in black women's historical romances. As historian Evelyn Higginbotham reminds us, "In societies where racial demarcation is endemic to their sociocultural fabric and heritage—to their laws and economy, to their institutionalized structures and discourses, and to their epistemologies and everyday customs—gender identity is inextricably linked to and even determined by racial identity."[19] Gender is racialized in black women's historical romances because black women have been historically and oftentimes ambivalently regarded as different from white women. In slavery, they were considered as beasts fit to lead a bestial life and as hot-tempered and immoral.[20] This racialized gender goes beyond Teresa de Lauretis's definition of gender, which she argues is "predicated on the conceptual and rigid (structural) opposition of the two biological sexes."[21] The variance in meanings is rooted in the inhumane and racist system of slavery that exploited black women's bodies and often caused friction in black male-female relationships.[22] The notion of the black woman as a body to be exploited persisted well into the nineteenth century. In the 1890s, for instance, Josephine St. Pierre Ruffin, a Boston activist, called a national convention of colored women after James W. Jacks, the white president of the Missouri Press Association, wrote a letter in 1895 accusing black women of having no character and no social credibility. In her manifesto, "A Call: Let Us Confer Together," Ruffin proposed the convening of the first national convention of colored women to educate the country to respect African American women.[23]

Black women's historical romances written from 1989 to the present alter and expand gender issues presented in the genre of their African American predecessors. Warding off gender attacks, the heroines subvert gratuitous sex between black women and white men that leads to pregnancy and motherhood in the novels of Frank Yerby.[24] While Yerby's type of relationship between a wealthy married white man and his groomed mulatta mistress may monetarily secure the black woman and her child for life, it debases the female and deadens opposition against race/gender/class biases. The second wave of black women's historical romances further expands gender issues presented in same-race unions found in nineteenth-century African American novels. Iola Leroy's doubts about her ability to pursue a public position as a married woman and Sappho Clark's apprehensions about Will Smith's desire for her as an unwed mother pale alongside the more confrontational issues found in late-twentieth-century historical romances.

In post-1989 novels, black women activists inveigh against, rather than acquiesce to, black patriarchy in the romance because it challenges their right to self-definition and their endeavors to uplift the race. They address historical problems related to the simultaneous ascendancy of black women and black men in the public sphere. After the Civil War, for instance, black men were expected to imitate the gender hierarchy found in white relationships, but this discriminatory paradigm caused conflict within black male-female relationships at a time when black women were emerging in their public roles. As black patriarchy struggled to maintain its own footing, it regarded black women's emerging roles as threats to black male positions in the community. The authoritative positions of black men contributed to and even complemented their sexist notions about woman's "place" in the home and in the community. In the nineteenth-century historical romances, black women censure those black men who seek to impose a prescriptive code of ethics concerning black womanhood. Despite the argument of Benjamin Quarles, a noted African American historian, that "black women were the first women in America to sit down with their men around political matters," some black men who rose to public positions themselves in the nineteenth century chastised the black woman for or interfered with her performance of public roles.[25]

The black female activist's response to black patriarchy often takes the form of defiant sexuality. In Jenkins's *Vivid*, Dr. Lancaster, the female physician, wears masculine attire (pants and work shirt) outlining the contours of her body as she affirms herself as female in the patriarchal town of Grayson Grove. In *Night Song*, Cara Henson, the teacher, becomes pregnant in her romantic relationship with Chase Jefferson, a cavalier soldier, but refuses to tell him about her parturiency. Fully aware of their need to assert the total self, these black women activists use sexuality as a weapon against chauvinism. Defiant sexuality evident in these novels sharply contrasts the frigidity of Mabelle Beaubean, alias Sappho Clark, in Pauline Hopkins's *Contending Forces* after her white uncle rapes her. When a black man discovers the assault to her virginity, Mabelle Beaubean reacts with "nervous spasms" and "disgrace" (30). Moreover, the issue of sexuality leading to consensual sex does not arise in same-race unions in Hopkins's and Harper's novels. Neither in Mabelle Beaubean's marriage to Will Smith nor in Iola Leroy's courtship by and marriage to Dr. Latimer is there mention of the black female's sexuality. Late-twentieth-century historical romances recount what conceivably did occur in the nineteenth century but what nineteenth-century black authors were too prudent to discuss owing to social convention. Then, too, sexuality in recent historical romances appeals to today's black female readers, who regard it as an important aspect of their self-definition.

In addition to gender bias, class prejudice proves to be another target for black women's activism in black women's historical romances. In African American culture, class bias is the handmaiden of intraracial prejudice that privileges the near-white or light-complexioned person over the darker-hued. Ingrained in the slave system, class bias was an insidious convention influenced by whites who made laws against educating slaves but often allowed for the education of the lighter-skinned subject. Sylvia Cannon, a Florence, South Carolina, slave, recalls that "the white folks didn't never help none of we black people to read and write no time. They learn the yellow chillun, but if they catch we black chillun with a book, they nearly 'bout kill us. They was sure better to them yellow chillun than the black chillun that be on the plantation."[26] According such a privilege to lighter-complexioned vassals gave the appearance of elevating those slaves' status above that of their illiterate darker-hued counterparts and psychologically sent the message to all that to be *black* was to be inferior. After the Civil War, the distinction that mulattoes made between themselves and their darker-hued counterparts led to what historian Eugene Genovese calls "a three-caste system," one that included whites, dark-skinned blacks, and a minority of haughty bourgeois mulattoes.[27] Prevalent in South Carolina, New Orleans, and Alabama, this third tier of mulattoes, separate from whites and the darker-hued blacks, became a superficial construct that deluded some slaveborn offspring of mixed-race parents and some light-complexioned freeborn blacks into thinking that they were indeed better off than their darker-hued brothers and sisters, whether they had formal education or not. Most southern whites, however, made no distinction between blacks and the mulattoes, variously referred to as "blue veins," "high yellows," and "red bones." To drive home their sense of importance, the less-educated mulattoes referenced their white bloodlines and often pretended to be more than they were. The more educated blue veins organized with the intent to uplift the impoverished, illiterate, and "inferior" darker members of the race, even if they did not always succeed. As teachers, doctors, and lawyers, they have historically been regarded as the black community's upper crust.

Black women's historical romances dramatize the reality of intracaste distinctions. The earlier novels of Harper and Hopkins assign class superiority to the educated mulatta. Iola Leroy, educated in the North, lauds herself over the slaves. Her arrogance stems from her erroneous beliefs that she is white and that "slaves do not want their freedom" (97–98). Post-1989 narratives, in contrast, attribute the higher social status to the darker-hued female and expose the superficiality of the lighter-hued characters who base their self-worth on color, bloodline, manners, and education. These latter narratives disprove the myth of dark-skinned women's inferior class status. In Beverly Jenkins's *Vivid*, for instance, the dark-skinned protagonist Dr. Viveca Lancaster is a medical physician from an upper-class background. A descendant of the Spanish Moors who founded Los Angeles, she contends with a group of self-serving near-whites who turn out to be nothing more than noisy busybodies. In Francine Craft's *The Black Pearl* (1996), Katherine, the dark-skinned protagonist, exhibits more benevolence toward those of her race than does Celie, her light-skinned, self-serving sister-in-law. Both women are descendants of slaves, but slaveborn Katherine denies herself to help others, whereas freeborn Celie uses her free birth, complexion, and herbalist trade to set herself apart from Katherine.

My third argument for reading black women's twentieth-century historical romances is to illuminate an Africana womanist[28] narratology as a model for understanding these black female-centered discourses. Such a narratology embraces specific tactics of activism used by black women in their struggles for self-actualization and communal advancement. Primary among these tactics, which Clenora Hudson-Weems outlines in her study *Africana Womanism: Reclaiming Ourselves* and which appear in African American women's historical romances, are self-naming, self-definition, family centeredness, working with black males in the freedom struggle, bonding in sisterhood, exhibiting strength, desiring male compatibility, demanding respect and recognition, seeking wholeness, and demonstrating spirituality.[29] These characteristics are prominent in women-centered narratives in which women's values and authority derive from womanist principles of narrative desire.[30] I therefore argue that an Africana womanist reading should be employed in the works of the five African American womanist writers in this study. These writers are reading their characters' desires and experiences and re-creating nineteenth-century and early-twentieth-century history in the romances. I use the term *Africana* advisedly to refer to black American women of African descent who have engaged in liberation struggles in America; therefore, in this study, the ethnic designations "black," "African American," and "Africana" are used interchangeably.

Womanism identifies the Africana woman as doer, the agent implementing communal wholeness. As an activist, she fights for the care and protection of others and the recognition and naming of herself as "woman." The term *womanism* in this study replaces "feminism." Despite some black women scholars' use of the term *feminism* to critically assess black women's struggles,[31] feminism as a term evolved long after black women's struggles began on American soil and is associated currently with middle-class white women's resistance against patriarchy and their desires to liberate themselves from the home, which they consider "a prison."[32] In the cultural tradition of African Americans, Africana women have worked with their men in the race struggle and have regarded their homes as a primary site of resistance. Moreover, throughout the nineteenth century and early twentieth century, which is the sociohistorical focus of this study, African American women referred to themselves as *women*, not feminists.[33] Sojourner Truth in her 1851 "Woman's Rights Speech" asked the militant and pertinent question, "And ain't I a Woman?"[34] Forty years later, Anna Julia Cooper in "The Status of Woman in America" (1892) wrote, "The colored woman of today occupies . . . a unique position in this country. In a period of itself transitional and unsettled, her status seems one of the least ascertainable and definitive of all forces which made for our civilization."[35] Truth and Cooper illuminate the bold public stand that black women took to define themselves and secure their status as women in America. Black women engaged themselves in an activism that embodied specific Africana womanist characteristics, as outlined by Clenora Hudson-Weems in *Africana Womanism*, that appear in African American women's historical romances. These characteristics are embedded in an Afrocentric ethos that supports the heroine's position as activist in the historical romances.

In addition, these womanist characters apply three other affirmative strategies to empower themselves in the face of sociohistorical oppression: expressive power, migratory power, and tentative sexual abstinence. Expressive power and migratory power are identified among the nine controls of strength accessible to the powerless in Bernice Carroll's essay "Peace Research: The Cult of Power."[36] *Expressive power* is venting discontent or rage at circumstances encountered, while *migratory power* refers to a self-imposed transference, although political and social issues may peripherally influence the displacement.[37] Expressive power and migratory power are typically used to vent dissatisfaction against race, gender, and class prejudices. In contrast to the polite, Christianlike rejection of injustices in nineteenth-century historical romances, late-twentieth-century narratives showcase uncivil, in-your-face discontent. In Beverly Jenkins's *Through the Storm*, Sable Fontaine lashes out at an illegal trafficker in slaves and tells him that despite his money, he is nothing but trash to her. Her anger unveils her unwillingness to be bought after slavery has been declared illegal. Migratory power is evident in all of the historical romances in this study; it decreases the opponents' targets and promises a better life for the heroines. Moreover, it continues the tradition of nineteenth-century narratives that chronicle the movements of blacks away from terrorist sites. The protagonist in each novel moves from one part of the country to another as an expression of self-determination. The distance traveled, though, takes the heroines in the novels of Bunkley and her successors farther than those in earlier narratives.

Owing to the particular nature of her race, gender, and class struggles, the black female protagonist-activist in post-1989 historical romances occasionally applies still another strategy of empowerment—sexual abstinence. A strategy directed at modifying the historical and social myth of black women's moral depravity, it strengthens the black female protagonist's traditionally assumed "weak" position in her interactions with "strong" men. Hester Wyatt, in Beverly Jenkins's *Indigo*, engages this tactic with Galen Vashon at the same time that she enhances her sexuality. A virgin scented with vanilla extract, she withholds sex for months in order to subdue him. Her zero tolerance for Galen's sexual promiscuity attaches to her mission the concept of noble purpose and comes with her realization that when sex is all that a man values, he has no incentive to be good. The tension between sex and sexuality dissipates only after the heroine gains confidence that her partner will value her as a person as well as a sexual partner.

My fourth argument is that black women's historical romances interpret black women's activism as engaging a culture that embraces what Elmer P. Martin and Joanne Mitchell Martin refer to as "the black helping tradition."[38] Rooted in the African kinship system and transplanted to American soil, the black helping tradition is the charitable and civil disposition of African Americans toward each other for human preservation and for social and racial progress and toward those outside the race who need assistance. This tradition was prevalent when the shackles of slavery had not yet fallen and when black women were beginning to fashion their public roles in the nineteenth century. Central to this African-centered culture is a "collective psychological space," which separates African Americans from white oppression and enables them "to generate a sense of worth, dignity, affiliation, and mutual support."[39]

In Bunkley's *Emily, the Yellow Rose*, the African-centered cultural practice of caring for and investing time with nonrelational kin creates the psychological space separating Emily, the protagonist, from white oppression in her adopted home. In this novel, Emily involves herself with work where she deems it is most needed.

Black women's historical novels of the second wave expand on the black helping tradition found in nineteenth-century narratives. They link the helping tradition to Africa in various ways, one of which is to have an African matriarch, as in Jenkins's *Through the Storm*, pass on the tradition to her American-born female relative. This kinship and cultural link between characters makes a stronger case for the survival of the African-based helping tradition in recent African American narratives than in nineteenth-century historical romances. In *Iola Leroy,* for instance, Iola goes to great lengths to help others as a nurse, teacher, and daughter, but her only connection to Africa resides in her avowal, "The best blood in my veins is African blood." In late-twentieth-century/twenty-first-century second wave narratives, black heroines' connection to their African roots and their participation in the cultural tradition of giving more firmly establish their identity and kinship. The identity of female characters, their historical placement and origins, is instrumental to their self-representational mission and value in these plots. As Peter Brooks asserts, "The question of what we are typically must pass through the question of where we are, which in turn is interpreted to mean, how did we get to be there?"[40]

The four aforementioned arguments apply to historical romances written by five African American women—Bunkley, Jenkins, Hailstock, Craft, and Gunn—whose black characters form the corpus of their works and provide the substance for the chapters that follow in this book.[41] In chapter 1, dealing with pre–Civil War activism, black women battle for freedom during the colonization and abolitionist movements, periods of their initial appearances in the American public sphere. In chapter 2, on Civil War activism, black women stabilize the black family to moderate poverty. In chapter 3, on postbellum activism, the black woman heals as herbalist and medical physician. In chapter 4, on post-Reconstruction activism, black women educate and demand to be educated. In chapter 5, on the early twentieth century, one black woman confronts the injustice that threatens the fundamental right of black landownership as she struggles to save her land. In the epilogue, the discussion continues on the relevance of black female activists in these narratives to the expansion of the canon of African American literature. Organized chronologically, the chapters of this book provide historical continuity in the critical reading of these narratives. This structural mode allows for uniformity in revisiting the social and historical milieu in which black women activists made their debut and contributions, reveals the expanding borders of the black female literary character, and illuminates her functional role in the given narrative plan. All in all, this study provides a solid historical-literary framework for a body of new narratives too often considered as pulp fiction and illuminates strategies for reading these works containing fictional representations of nineteenth-century and early-twentieth-century black women who choose to act.

1 Antebellum Activism

The Call to Freedom

Emily, the Yellow Rose; *Nowhere to Run*; and *Indigo*

Maria Stewart began her "Lecture Delivered at the Franklin Hall" in Boston, September 21, 1832, with these militant words: "Why sit ye here and die? If we say we will go to a foreign land, the famine and pestilence are there, and there we shall die. If we sit here, we shall die. Come let us plead our cause before the whites: if they save us alive, we shall live—and if they kill us, we shall but die."[1] Stewart's vibrant words voiced her call for freedom and conveyed the idea that blacks must energize themselves to participate in their survival. Her speech resounded during two important pre–Civil War movements—colonization and abolitionism.

The colonization movement began in 1816 with the establishment of the American Colonization Society under President James Monroe, a southerner. This society established a settlement in Liberia to rid the South of the so-called troublesome free Negro, to provide a place for Negroes captured in the illegal slave trade, and to offer a supposedly humanitarian out for slave masters who wanted to rid themselves of their slaves.[2] The abolitionist movement officially began on January 1, 1831, with the initial publication of William Lloyd Garrison's weekly *The Liberator*, and flourished with the subsequent emergence of the New England Anti-Slavery Society (1832) and the American

Anti-Slavery Society (1833). The gradual and conciliatory movement to rid America of slavery in the 1830s transformed to a more immediate and militant one in the 1850s as black women moved to the forefront of this movement with strong supporters in Harriet Tubman, Sojourner Truth, Frances Ellen Watkins Harper, and Mary Ellen Pleasant. Both movements offered and challenged liberty, and some black women pleaded their causes to colonization agents and to abolitionists. For their activism, they sometimes found themselves simultaneously free and enslaved. Their predicament intensified their struggles.

Anita Richmond Bunkley's *Emily, the Yellow Rose* (1989), Gay G. Gunn's *Nowhere to Run* (1997), and Beverly Jenkins's *Indigo* (1996) celebrate black women responding to the freedom call via either colonization or abolitionism in the tradition of Harriet Tubman and Sojourner Truth. Heroines in these novels participate in two movements that heretofore have gone unexamined in black women's fiction. They take leading roles in predominantly male movements and function in these novels as primary opponents in race-based struggles rather than as auxiliary agents to men. The strength of these heroines exceeds that of their literary antecedents, especially Iola Leroy in Harper's *Iola Leroy*, who functions as an auxiliary to men during the Civil War, and Clotel in William Wells Brown's *Clotel*, who is a trapped, helpless fugitive slave. The second wave of historical romances features heroines who possess the strength and fortitude to subdue the opponent and effect change in the community.

The difference in the portrayal of heroines in the historical romances of Bunkley, Gunn, and Jenkins and those of nineteenth-century writers proceeds from the authors' use of race. In the tradition of nineteenth-century African American literature, race is used as an unjust separator of humanity in America and when attached to blacks is perceived as an affliction to avoid. Because race divides blacks from whites and alienates the former group from the privileges freely enjoyed by the latter, factionalism ensues. Characters in nineteenth-century African American historical romances are created in the images of the oppressor race and the mulatta employed to garner sympathy for the condition of the oppressed blacks. Her light skin tone becomes a weapon in the race war. Ironically, mulattas become more susceptible to gender abuse and class discrimination. Rebellion through flight thwarts their attempt to selfhood, and they either face the reality of their racial condition or die.

Black women writers of twentieth-century historical novels of the second wave use their race difference as an affirmation for nation building. Their characters eschew appeals to whites for better treatment through masks of light skin tones. Except for Bunkley's novel, which functions as a bridge between nineteenth-century and late-twentieth-century narratives, heroines are of dark complexions in post-1989 historical romances. They stand their ground as people of color to undo the stigma attached to their race.

Gender becomes a metaphor for black women's empowerment, even though gender has racial implications. Darker-hued heroines avoid or escape sexual abuse from white men, but they have gender confrontations with black men who attempt to control their bodies and influence their thinking in romantic relationships. The black woman's relationship to the white man and the black man in these novels is the reverse of what it is in nineteenth-century historical romances. This counterdepiction of black heroines enables them to apply womanist strategies of strength, trust, and intraracial togetherness. They work with their mates in the struggle against racial oppression at the same time that they build a life for themselves as strong public figures.

Race and gender influence class. Belonging to two minority groups, the heroines, as blacks and as women, are circumscribed to poverty. Their placement on the lower rung of the economic ladder is simply an eternal manifestation of a societally imposed social standing. Black women politicize their economic hardship by helping others to achieve freedom, and in so doing they redefine class to mean the worth assigned to a black woman who engages in work advantageous to the uplift of the race.

Situated in an overarching plot that offers maternal tropes and masculine-like heroism, heroines in these second wave narratives deliver other women to freedom, give birth to their own children, and deliver themselves to a state of fulfillment. Their masculinized heroism enables them to migrate great distances and engage in autonomous emancipative acts. Marriage fails to abort their political struggle for selfhood. The heroines' movements to sites of abolition or colonization signal their cancellation of an unproductive and marginal "other" status and their entrance into productive womanhood. What is more important is that female protagonists provide the reader with the grounds for understanding the race/gender/class conflict they encounter and the value system they embody in female-gendered character plots.

Anita Richmond Bunkley's *Emily, the Yellow Rose*

Privately printed in 1989,[3] *Emily, the Yellow Rose* captures a black woman's migration to Texas, the author's adopted state. Set during a tumultuous period in Texas history—its colonization and subsequent independence from Mexican rule—the novel links the black protagonist's travel to this foreign land to her activist search for full citizenship and personal freedom. Because few black women lived in Texas in the 1830s and because their actions, except for their performance of slave duties, have been historically recorded as inconsequential, *Emily, the Yellow Rose* has special significance. As noted earlier, as an historical romance it functions as a bridge between second wave narratives and African American women's nineteenth-century historical romances, a point that will be elaborated on later in this chapter. As a political document, it dramatizes the plight of a free black woman who resists race, gender, and class prejudices in this Southwest territory that simultaneously struggles for its own independence. A brief look at Texas history regarding blacks in the 1820s and 1830s will precede a discussion of the work as a political and literary document.

The events occurring in Texas in the 1820s and 1830s highlight the differences in political views that Mexicans and white Texans had about blacks, including mulattas, and announce the downside of Texas as a colonization site. At the seat of these differences was the dark issue of slavery, which inevitably touched the lives of free blacks who migrated to this territory. On July 13, 1824, thirteen years after its independence from Spain, Mexico prohibited "commerce and traffic in slaves . . . proceeding from any country and under any flag whatsoever."[4] Anglos debated whether the Mexican government intended the law to cease the importation of all bondsmen for trade or whether it intended to prohibit slave owners from bringing their chattel into the territory. Anglos and others who had come with their slaves from southern states and had settled in various communities in Texas such as San Felipe de Austin[5] and Washington on the Brazos[6] made every effort to skirt the law. Ultimately, Anglos evaded the law prohibiting slavery. They insisted on black labor for the expansion of their colonies and the development of the cotton fields and sugar plantations, and they forced their slaves to indenture themselves for years by signing irrevocable contracts. James Morgan, for instance, bound his slaves for ninety-nine years; the males were instructed to farm and plant and the females to cook and keep house.[7] Marmaduke D. Sandifer entered into a contract with Clarissa, a colored woman, at San Felipe de Austin, according to which she promised to give up her liberty and serve her master faithfully for ninety-nine years.[8] Black women who were *de jure* free on Mexico's soil were *de facto* slaves of whites who themselves revolted against the Mexicans to gain their own independence in the Battle of San Jacinto, April 21, 1836.[9]

Texas's fight for independence and for legalized slavery coincided with the struggle of free blacks nationwide to pursue freedom and full citizenship status. Full citizenship meant freedom from random attacks brought about by whites' fear of slave uprisings and by the growing free black population. Many states restricted manumission, limited the rights of free blacks, forced them to reenslave themselves, and expelled them to or induced them to settle in remote areas. Texas, as a distant frontier, was recognized during the 1830s as a viable locale to colonize free blacks. Benjamin Lundy, a well-known abolitionist, deemed Texas as more suitable than Liberia to establish a free black colony, and he traveled to that frontier three times for that purpose.[10] And Nicholas Drouett, a mulatto and associate of Lundy's, scouted Texas unsuccessfully for places to settle five hundred Negro families.[11] While neither Lundy's nor Drouett's schemes to colonize free blacks succeeded, the Mexican chargé d'affaires at Washington, with the sanction of the Mexican government, made it clear to all blacks in America that if they resided in Texas, they would have equal rights, lands, implements for farming, and protection to pursue their work undisturbed.[12]

Free blacks migrated to Texas in the 1830s either with the help of white individuals or upon answering advertisements by land companies headed by real estate developers. White men promised blacks citizenship and passports, but their prime aim was to better their own economic circumstances, expand Anglo colonies, and further the war effort against Mexico. Free black women worked in Texas as cooks, kitchen helpers, and washerwomen, and black men as laborers. Free black women who migrated to Texas in the 1830s included Harriett Newell Sands, who came with Mr. Manton from Michigan in 1834; Zelia Husk, who migrated from Georgia and settled in Houston in 1838 as a laundress; and Diana Leonard,[13] after whom a character in *Emily, the Yellow Rose* is named, who came to Texas in 1835 and worked for one year in the household of Colonel James Morgan. These free black women worked alongside slaves passed off as indentured servants, and their circumstances proved to be little better than those of slave women.

As a political document, *Emily, the Yellow Rose* has significance. It intersects the struggle of a free black woman for self-definition on Mexican soil with the Anglos' struggle for independence from Mexico. As a result of these struggles, two ironies evolve. The novel reveals the inherent discrepancy between America's identity as a democracy and its execution of undemocratic principles toward blacks, and it manifests the imperialistic ideas of the white majority who as a minority on foreign soil disobey Mexican laws and overthrow the ruler. In both instances, race is present. Hostilities that afflicted blacks and whites in the mainland United States are transferred to the colonial wilderness. And the idea of color superiority is transferred, too, in the interaction between whites and Mexicans.

The novel uses legend and Texas history to construct the story of protagonist Emily West, named after Emily D. West, the mulatta who inspired the African American folk ballad "The Yellow Rose of Texas."[14] According to the ballad, Emily, a mulatta, more beautiful than the "belles of Tennessee," is separated from her lover, a "darky," who searches for her. Legend has it that Mexican general Antonio Lopez de Santa Anna kidnapped Emily D. West from the Morgan settlement, which had been fortified with U.S. soldiers. She later detained him in his tent while Texans defeated his troops at San Jacinto in 1836 and won their independence from Mexico.

Historians disagree about Emily D. West's identity. This disagreement essentially revolves around Emily's origins and legal status. Historian Martha Anne Turner identifies Emily as an indentured servant, the one Colonel Morgan brought from New York in 1835 to work in his household at New Washington. It was this slave girl, Turner asserts, who later related to Colonel

Morgan how Santa Anna forcibly took her from the Morgan house and how she survived Sam Houston's attack on Santa Anna's forces at San Jacinto.[15] Stephen Harrigan believes that Emily was a staff member in the household of James Morgan, a merchant from North Carolina and a Texas real estate developer.[16] David A. Williams recognizes Emily D. West as the slave of Colonel James K. Morgan,[17] who "brought [her] to Texas from New York in 1835."[18] He affirms that Emily was born a "West" but later assumed her master's surname. Margaret Swett Henson writes that Emily "was not a slave, her last name was not Morgan . . . [she did not] delay Santa Anna in his tent . . . [and there is no] evidence to connect Emily with the popular nineteenth-century ballad, 'The Yellow Rose of Texas.'"[19] Randolph B. Campbell adroitly admits that no basis for the legend exists. He offers that Emily was not a slave and that no evidence supports Emily's presence among the slaves that James Morgan brought to Texas in 1831 or owned in Texas. Campbell connects Emily D. West to Emily West de Zavala of New York, who brought with her to Texas in 1831 a servant girl named Emily D. West. It was this servant girl, Campbell maintains, that Santa Anna captured when the de Zavala family sought refuge at the Morgan home.[20]

Historians' debate over Emily D. West's identity no doubt stems from the ambiguity of blacks' status at that historical time. The state of New York had legally freed its slaves on July 4, 1827, and, therefore, Emily was a free black woman whether she left New York in 1831 or 1835 to come to Texas. Her migration to Texas to work in an Anglo household that had converted its slaves to indentured servants in order to subvert Mexican law barring slavery essentially made her indistinguishable from the remainder of the slaves in that household. Thus Campbell's conclusion that Emily's "story bears no relationship to slavery in Texas because Emily West was always a free woman"[21] misconstrues a certain reality—free black women in Anglo Texas in 1835 did not enjoy a life separate and distinct from that of slave women. Mexican law did not discriminate against any person for reason of birth or color, but Anglos in Texas did. According to historian C. R. Wharton, "the provisional government and the Republic were very antagonistic to free negroes, and they were denied residence [in Brazoria, an early Anglo settlement]."[22] Wharton's conclusion certainly confirms why some African Americans actually had to petition Congress to be permitted to remain in the state.

Despite the varied opinions about Emily D. West's identity, the central character in *Emily, the Yellow Rose* is Emily West, a young, unmarried, free black female protagonist who migrates from New York to Texas. Bunkley's choice of such a main character is no doubt to illuminate the conflicts a free black woman encountered on this supposedly opportunistic frontier. Basing her story on the African American folk legend that the historical Emily inspired and incorporating the incident of San Jacinto as the climax of her novel, Bunkley localizes her protagonist's personal struggles with race, gender, and class oppression in this political record.

In its capacity as a bridge between the historical romances written by nineteenth-century African Americans and those of the second wave, the novel's obvious link to the former is the skin tone of the heroine. A refined mulatta, Emily recalls nineteenth-century mulattas such as Harper's Minnie and Iola Leroy, Hopkins's Sappho Clark, and Brown's Clotel. Emily's skin color, however, is not used as a mask to appeal to whites for equality. Instead, Emily's skin color indicates a race difference that aligns its bearer with the oppressed minority group. Her obvious protest against racism connects her as a character to the dark-skinned heroines in post-1989 historical novels.

Nineteenth-century mulattas evolved in a literary tradition in which authors insisted upon the humanity of African Americans by casting their characters in the image of whites, whom history regarded as a superior race and from whom the fictional characters sought justice. As a literary convention, mulatta characters often moved at the will of the oppressor. Their passage from one location to another was motivated by force and fear, rather than by discontent. They had little connection to an African heritage or to the African-derived helping tradition. In their journeys, their aid to others is based on duty and convenience. Iola, for instance, dutifully searches for her mother and attends to wounded soldiers; Sappho returns to the South to care for the small son she has abandoned; and Clotel helps William to escape because she needs him for her own flight. Mulattas often appear in conventional plots wherein woman and man meet, fall in love, and marry. The heroines usually encounter gender abuse from white men and do not participate in same-race lovemaking, and their marriages end their usefulness as public figures. They do not function in maternal plots because they are deprived of a sustained social struggle that produces a public birth.

Earlier writers established and populated the African American literary canon with mulattas, their friends, and families as a polemic convention, but Bunkley takes the mulatta from African American legend, shaped by the vagaries of history, and reshapes her as a plausible, strong character in the historical context in which she is found. Emily is a loner with no family; her decision to migrate is based on a desire for upward mobility, and this desire is made known early in the novel. Her complexion and family background are secondary to her actions. Her decision to make an individual strike against racism during an important period in American history aligns her with the darker heroines prominent in the second wave of historical romances. Her bold personal strike for freedom metaphorically signals the beginning of an important womanhood wherein decisive and masculine-like action is demonstrated.

Emily's tale is constructed in a woman-centered character plot with an overarching structure of malelike will and fortitude. This plot contains three distinct phases that simulate the maturation of a female from infertility to motherhood. The novel begins with the virginal or nonproductive stage, wherein the longing heroine desires a change, and proceeds with the insemination and subsequent gestational phases that reveal the protagonist's tensions and stresses of a mock gravidity. It closes open ended with the birth of a new life. As a character plot with this maternal thread, *Emily, the Yellow Rose* has a time frame of nine months dating from summer 1835 until April 1836, corresponding with the conflict between the Anglos and the Mexicans. This chronology aids a female-centered reading of the novel and complements what narratologist Paul Ricoeur refers to as a "time-dependent" narrative. Such a saga has three temporal periods: (1) the "prefiguration" stage in which the individual desires change, (2) the "figuration" or action time in which the protagonist struggles to effect an outcome, and (3) the "refiguration" stage that gives a retrospective consideration of actions and unexpected effects.[23] These three junctures are evident in *Emily, the Yellow Rose*, and each presages the protagonist's resistance to social and historical protocol.

The virginal (prefiguration) stage vividly depicts Emily West's desire for change. A northern, free mulatta, she is dissatisfied with her second-class citizenship in New York City. A woman of few words, she has lived quietly in New York trying to avoid any explosive situation. Regarding herself as an American entitled to full citizenship when America sees her only as a second-class citizen, Emily's goal is to write herself into history as a full citizen. Her strong character merges with her desire to secure the maternal foundation of a home and settle comfortably. A fictional prototype, Emily represents a class of blacks whose security was severely threatened nationwide during the 1830s when many were kidnapped and remanded to slavery or killed. She symbolizes one of the approximately 10 percent, or roughly 389,195, of free blacks living prior to the Civil War[24] and one of the approximately 150 blacks residing in Texas at the time of Texas's independence.[25]

Emily's vicarious insemination and gestation (figuration stage) are initiated by the Union Land Company agent who functions as male copula and pays Emily's passage to the province for her to work as a cook. The insemination comes with sweet promises—a new home, a passport, and a certification of freedom. The evil intent inherent in the patriarchal allure—the agent places Emily aboard the schooner *Exert* (a phallic symbol) with manacled slaves en route to Texas—conflicts with Emily's womanist desire for fulfillment. Her migration illuminates the moral consciousness that shapes her character as an activist and her willingness to stretch her being for growth. At the depth of Emily's existence is the knowledge that disenfranchisement based on race is a moral wrong. Her desire for full citizenship, even in another country, corresponds to her urgent need for the God-given right to self-definition. Given the historical climate and the fact that she has neither family nor husband to depend on, her decision to give up her job as a teacher's assistant to move to Texas seems to her to be the best solution to the race problem. In fact, when she reaches Texas, she feels as though she were home.

In her new home, Emily experiences the discomforts of her "first trimester." Her emotions waver from satisfaction to anger as she develops morning sickness from an oppressive social and historical gestation. Her immediate annoyance stems from two white males, Clabe Ledbetter, a white soldier in Sam Houston's army, and John Reese,[26] a businessman. Together, they represent institutionalized racism in Texas, and use epithets to illustrate racial difference. They refer to blacks as "niggers" and "nigras." Their language demonstrates what Tracey E. Ore refers to as "a powerful tool of culture, determining how members of a society interpret their environment."[27] Ledbetter and Reese interpret their environment as a racially constructed world in which whites maintain and exercise an ideology of white supremacy and black inferiority.

Emily's awareness of her racial conflict with these men escalates to personal feelings about intersecting gender and class differences and makes her wonder if her decision to come to Texas had been an error. Clabe, for instance, tosses Emily's document of freedom on the ground after he capriciously cuts off a lock of her hair and threatens to take her home with him if she does not possess free papers. In addition, he searches her person for money and books.

This first public humiliation provides Emily the occasion to rebel, and she does. She assumes a militant stance. She looks Clabe in the eye and jerks her head backward in anger. Emily's kinetic response comes as she wishes the hatred in her eyes to mirror her disgust. Her anger manifests the depth of her thinking about the immorality of race and gender prejudice and proves her courage to act if pushed. Anger, described by Christa Reiser as the emotion between "havoc and hope," certainly applies to Emily's conflicting circumstances.[28] Emily's anger comes with the realization that her desire (hope) for equality in Texas conflicts with the ideology (havoc) of the dominant white power structure. Her response magnifies the capriciousness of white injustice and reveals her firm belief in protecting what is hers and in maintaining dignity and freedom. Her bold reactions, even when mixed with fear and trembling, metaphorically represent the beginning of several bouts of nausea she will encounter in her mock pregnancy.

Emily's discomfort in the first trimester comes with her ignorance about the implications of the migration. What she does not know and what the land agent does not tell her is that the Mexican territory of Texas is preparing for an impending war against whites who have settled in the province, many with their slaves, and that whites in the area are drafting soldiers and recruiting black labor to shore up their defenses during wartime. Unaware of what she has gotten herself into, she gains the reader's sympathy and reflects the dashed hopes of young women riding on the belly of masculine allure. She did not expect her new life to be in such a dismal place with dirt roads and no shops. Her ignorance merges with maternal images of heat and water to further add to her distress. Perspiration pours down the back of her dress, causing her extreme discomfort in the heat. Settling in the Gulf Coastal Plain of eastern/southeastern Texas, which experiences long periods of rain, Emily is also depressed by frequent downpours mixed with mud. Significantly, her unsuspecting character recalls the trust of many unprotected blacks who migrated to foreign areas in the nineteenth century and too soon experienced disappointment.

The "second trimester" reveals Emily's struggles for growth as a person. Her development merges with the intensified Mexican-Anglo conflict. The map preceding the narrative establishes the physical geography of this antagonistic area about which Emily gains more knowledge and in which the advancing armies led by Sam Houston and Santa Anna confront each other. The map charts the movement of both armies across several rivers (San Antonio, Guadalupe, Colorado, Brazos, and San Jacinto) and bullets the towns of Goliad, San Antonio, Matagorda, San Felipe, Harrisburg, and New Washington, the latter of which is where Emily settles and where she offers the most resistance.[29] Outlining an area with a mixed terrain of water and land that changes to mud after heavy rains, the map symbolically weds Texas's shifting terrain to its unsteady sociopolitical climate and to Emily's alternating states of fear and wonder. The architectural blend of unsteady soil and uncertain politics places Emily West in a quagmire of circumstances that challenge her free status.

The muddy terrain concretizes Emily's descent from her free status. En route to New Washington where her job as a cook awaits her, Emily rides in a wagon that sinks in rank underbrush. Mired in mud, the carriage shifts its weight. The shift metaphorically foreshadows Emily's unexpected change in her status—based on race, gender, and class difference—from a free black woman to an enslaved black "wench." Reese, the driver, facilitates this shift by transporting the frustrated and disappointed Emily with other blacks at night to the Morgan Plantation, called Orange Grove.[30] At the Morgan Plantation in New Washington, Emily works on a dirt-floor kitchen alongside Hannah, a slave who prepares food for soldiers in Sam Houston's army housed on Colonel James Morgan's plantation. On this sinking soil, blacks—enslaved, indentured, and free—hold no distinction from each other, because many whites make no distinction.

Emily's descent from a free black occurs at night, and the darkness reveals her tormented inner consciousness. In a disturbed sleep, she encounters barking dogs chasing her. Dreaming that her legs are shackled and that the landscape has changed from prairie grass to swamp trees, Emily subconsciously embodies the reality of her dire situation. Coming after Emily's discussion with slave Hannah, who inquires why she came to Texas when she could reside as a free person in the North, the dream plunges Emily into the depths of despair and isolation and causes her for the second time to question her decision to come to Texas. The strength of Emily's character is observed when she wipes away tears and mentally and physically prepares herself to start a new day.

In darkness, Emily resists gender abuse. In the dark storage room on the Morgan Plantation, she fights with Clabe, who attempts unsuccessfully to rape her. She knees him, bites his lip, and yanks his head back—defensive masculine maneuvers that goad him on until Celia Morgan, Emily's employer, intervenes. Despite Emily's bold defense, her ultimate vulnerability shows when Clabe succeeds in raping her on his second try in the dark of a cavernous canebrake on swampy ground. The place where Clabe rapes Emily and the reason why he rapes her merge geography with sociopolitical attitudes. His belief that Emily is just another black woman who should respond to his sexual appetite typifies the white man's thinking about black women on this southern frontier and violates everything that Emily represents. Moreover, Clabe's beliefs embody race, gender, and class difference and, when exercised at night, encapsulate the evil of racism that Emily struggles against.

Although a malevolent force that nurtures race, gender, and class oppression, darkness also brings hope. It provides the setting for the courtship of Emily and Joshua Kinney, a freeborn, banjo-playing medicine man and son of a Creek woman. Emily believes that Joshua is a kind, just man, and her estimate of him is correct. Their first meeting occurs on the rutted path to the Morgan Plantation when Joshua emerges out of the darkness to help John Reese extricate the wagon from the mud. Emily meets him again when he comes to her dark cabin to attend to the ill Diana,[31] who eventually dies. In the dark, Joshua proves how much he loves Emily by killing Clabe on the Morgan Plantation when Clabe attacks Emily for the third time. And in the darkness, Joshua flees from evil after Emily sends word to him that bounty hunters are tracking him for allegedly instigating an insurrection. Darkness allows the lovers the psychological space to support each other in a geographical setting that robs them as minorities of their physical space.

Emily's support of Joshua and her care of Diana identify her as a participant in the black helping tradition. Devoting unselfish help to others relieves her of her gestational discomfort and aids her in her mock second trimester. She employs her cabin as an external manifestation of her benevolence. Elevated above the ground and consisting of two crudely constructed beds with straw mattresses, the cabin is the site of support and resistance, and it offers Emily and Joshua the psychological space to distance themselves from the region's oppression. Cultural sharing, ministrations, and nurturance are housed in this cabin and are requisite for Emily's dignity and support to others. In this small, cramped space, Emily nurses the sick Diana and sequesters and tends to Joshua after Clabe shoots him. A site of resistance, the cabin also provides the lovers a space to consummate their love. A place to heal, love, rest, and affirm their lives, the small cabin becomes the brief psychological haven from the physical boundaries imposed by the Texas frontier and from the emotional stress that has caused Emily to realize that to whites, she has the same status as the field hands and, as a black woman, is not worthy to breathe the same air as whites.

In this psychological space, Emily draws upon her gender strength. A sensuous woman, she responds to Joshua's passion differently from the way she responded to Clabe's. With her long, black hair flowing around her shoulders, she closes her eyes to revel in Joshua's lovemaking. Consistent with prior actions, Emily delves into this new adventure before knowing all the facts. She engages in sex with Joshua without knowing whether or not he is a runaway. Even so, Emily is not a loose woman. Her premarital rashness comes with a deep feeling for Joshua, a moral responsibility, and a class ethic to marry. Her shopping for a white lace mantilla that makes her feel elegant best describes her marriage intentions.

Despite the love that Emily has for Joshua, the impending war affects her relationship with him and alters Joshua's character. A hunted person, Joshua misuses what little power he has against Emily. Employing the traditional masculine strategy of evasion to maintain his control in the relationship, Joshua ignores Emily's questions about his origin and avoids her queries concerning his whereabouts. Emily knows nothing of his decision to flee and expects his return for several months. Despite Joshua's masculine brashness, Emily empowers herself in the relationship and aids Joshua, who is unable to help himself. Conferring with her liberal mistress, Emily secures for Joshua a safe place at New Washington from bounty hunters. And, on another occasion, she persuades Joshua to return to New Washington instead of heading to Refugio, Mexico, after she receives news from a white woman about Santa Anna's destruction of nearby western towns. Emily's warning affirms her disenchantment with a racist environment that keeps Joshua on the run and that limits her and him, as free people, in their romantic relationship. Assuming that she cannot change her environment, she changes her position in the relationship with Joshua by making arrangements for his safekeeping rather than vice versa. Her new position in the relationship shows her willingness to work with her man in the race struggle as she achieves gender empowerment.

In her "third trimester," Emily gains strength and weight as she assumes responsibility for the care of the Morgan Plantation after Colonel Morgan and his wife Celia take shelter on Galveston Island. Through her take-charge actions, Emily exhibits strength of character, distinguishing herself from the weak-spirited slave Hannah. She loses patience with Hannah and orders her to stop babbling her fears about the impending Mexican invasion. At the core of Emily's belief is that the work they have to do should keep them from thinking about the war. Like Hannah, Emily is afraid of what the war will bring, but she subordinates her fear to a higher purpose—securing slave women and children in the big house and feeding white women and their children who have sought shelter at the Morgan Plantation.

In an act of bravery, Emily refuses to escape when Santa Anna's army advances on New Washington. She stays at the Morgan Plantation to fulfill her promise to protect Celia Morgan's home. Her decision endangers her life, but to her the value of her word to another means everything.

Emily's "labor" occurs with her capture as Santa Anna's booty. Gagged, tied, and tossed across his horse with her head toward the ground, Emily experiences severe discomfort. The jolting movements of the horse parallel the later motions of Santa Anna, who rapes Emily in his tent. Emily retaliates for the sexual attack with adverse political consequences for Santa Anna.[32] Refusing to awaken the Mexican general to alert him to Sam Houstón's advance on the Mexican camp during siesta, Emily presents victory to Texas. Her actions present her as the first character in African American literature to become an agent for Texas independence.

Stephen Harrigan refers to Emily as the "accidental heroine" of Texas independence.[33] From a gender perspective, however, it is more reasonable to argue that Emily consciously and rationally seized the appropriate moment of patriarchal weakness to reassert her gender strength. Her assessment of the capability of Sam Houston's army was far superior to that of Santa Anna, who held only disdain for the poorly disciplined and badly equipped men in Houston's outfit.[34] That she stayed awake, rather than succumb to a drowsy stupor after her rape, proves her greater physical endurance after the sexual attack. Her actions voice her strength as a woman and her desire to free her total self. Rather than an "accidental heroine," Emily can more appropriately be referred to as an *activist* in this new frontier.

The narrative's third phase (birth or "refiguration") occurs at the site of the burning Morgan home to which Emily flees. With the disposal of Orange Grove comes an intense release of all the disappointment and anger she has experienced since her journey to Texas. The expulsion, viewed by Emily as another beginning, arrives with a brief retrospective consideration of all that has passed. Her conclusion that it is pointless to return to Orange Grove reveals a weary but undefeated Emily. Her reference to the unlivability of the land is a scathing indictment of the colonization movement that lured hopeful blacks into dismal territories. At its worst, colonization is seen as an immoral scheme by greedy agents to rid America of African Americans without giving a second thought to their welfare.

Emily's decision to strike out as an individual against racism during an important period in American history aligns her with the darker-skinned heroines prominent in the second wave of historical romances. Her bold personal strike for freedom metaphorically signals the beginning of an important womanhood, wherein decisive action, a display of sexuality, and physical force are exerted. Emily, the activist, blends ladylike strategies with masculine tactics. Silent rejection merges with kicks and bites. Her pivotal position between nineteenth-century mulatta characters and her own dark-skinned contemporaries firmly establishes *Emily, the Yellow Rose* as the initial novel of the second wave of African American women's historical romances.

Bunkley's carefully crafted tale keeps alive the memory of a pioneer black woman activist who in seeking full citizenship found challenges to her goal. Linking her protagonist to Emily D. West, the historical mulatta who inspired the folk ballad "The Yellow Rose of Texas," Bunkley replenishes the racial connection that time has eroded from the song. By 1955, according to Stephen Harrigan, "the song was an all-purpose Texas anthem, suitable for use in Ralph Yarborough's Senate campaign and Butter Krust bread commercials."[35]

Gay G. Gunn's *Nowhere to Run*

Gunn's 1997 novel is anchored in the historic moment of the 1840s Gold Rush. It is partially based on the life of Mary Ellen Pleasant (1814–1904), cook, entrepreneur, and abolitionist. Affectionately known as "Mammy Pleasant," she was born free in Philadelphia, according to her memoirs, although some historians say that she was born a slave in Georgia.[36] She married Alexander Smith, a wealthy planter from Cuba, and settled in Boston where they opened their home to abolitionists. Upon Smith's death, she married John Pleasant, with whom she migrated from the East Coast to California during the 1840s Gold Rush.[37] In San Francisco, where she settled, her activist strategies were planned in the kitchen of her boardinghouses and restaurants. She aided and abetted fugitives, challenged Jim Crow codes, fought for blacks' right to testify in court, and participated in various other community affairs. Because of her outspokenness, she became a victim of character distortion in press releases. Called a voodoo queen and a madam, she chose to ignore others' opinions about her. A strong-willed, proud, intuitive, affectionate, and giving person, Mary Ellen Pleasant, in an autobiographical essay, sums up her own individuality: "If a write-up of me put an extra blanket on somebody's bed or gave a household meat and bread, I would let them lay my character down in the middle of the road and let the whole world jump on it, and then turn it over and let them go [sic] it again."[38] Her assessment of herself sums up her humanitarianism, self-esteem, and risk taking. These were Pleasant's dominant traits as an activist, and these become the prominent characteristics of Cassie Lee, her fictional counterpart and heroine in *Nowhere to Run.*

Similar to Emily West in *Emily, the Yellow Rose,* Cassie Lee moves through three phases in Gay G. Gunn's novel—infertility (prefiguration), gestation (figuration), and motherhood (refiguration). In these three phases, she manifests her activism in conflicting race/gender/class situations. What she says and does and what others say about her in her confrontational circumstances reveal her evolving character. Cassie Lee evolves from a woman speaking for herself to one speaking for others as she progresses from a slave to a free woman, from a molested female to a willing and consensual wife. Her maturation is made evident through her risk taking, her insistence on self-esteem, and her humanitarianism.

In the infertility (prefiguration) stage, Cassie Lee takes a risk. Unlike Emily, the free mulatta virgin of Bunkley's novel, Cassie Lee is a brown-skinned sexually molested slave, determined to leave the Georgia plantation. She takes a risk when she leaves with Solomon Hawk, a black slave broker with gold to barter for her sale. She wagers on the unknown instead of the known. Figuring she will soon die from resisting her young white master, who sexually assaults her at night, she volunteers to go with Hawk to the Sierra Nevada to join with Exum Taylor, a man she does not know. Her decision to migrate manifests her resistance to slavery and her desire for freedom and a family of her own. Before she leaves, she wants assurance from Hawk that she will become Exum's wife, not his slave. Cassie Lee's insistence upon an answer encapsulates her wish for a better life as a female.

Voicing her expectation of homemaking, Cassie Lee politicizes her right as a woman to have her own home. She protests the white South's denial of the black woman's autonomy in her home and the separation of the black family in slavery. The pre–Civil War South's denial of Cassie Lee's right to a legal husband, home, and children culminates in her migration as a form of race/gender/class protest. To rise above the inferiority of her black slave status, the young master's defilement of her gender, and the lowliness of her class, Cassie Lee looks to the North and West to become the wife of Exum Taylor, owner of Exum Town, and keeper of his home. At the heart of her protest is her need to repair her damaged identity as a poor black female.

A description of what Cassie Lee looks like reveals what she is not. A tall, thin, attractive, black-haired woman with a honey complexion, Cassie Lee may be the object of her master's lust, but she is not a willing whore. Her sensuous facade—high cheekbones, full lips, and intelligent doe eyes—differs from the stereotypic depiction of the vacuous and lascivious slave woman. Rather than rely on her good looks to achieve self-definition, Cassie Lee exercises her intuition.

The narrative progresses to the second, or gestational, phase of the maternal plot after Hawk, representing the phallic symbol, vicariously plants in Cassie Lee the freedom seed. This stage brings considerable gender upset and produces unsettling results. Ironically, the gender abuse Cassie Lee has experienced at the hands of her slave master is about to recur in her relationship with Exum Taylor, who wants Cassie Lee as his prostitute, not his wife. Protesting Exum's wish to control her body, Cassie Lee aborts the connection between racism and sexism that Exum, as an ex-slave, has seized as a means to bring value to himself. Protesting gender abuse, Cassie Lee resolves not to become another man's slave. Her resistance to Exum reiterates the strength of her character and metaphorically induces symptoms of a mock pregnancy. She becomes flushed and mortified to find that home with Exum, her husband-to-be, means a saloon in which he expects her to work as a prostitute. She rejects the gaudy clothes that Exum expects her to wear, and is dismayed that a two-story home with curtains at the windows is not present for her to settle in. Cassie Lee's expectations exceed reality, and when she discovers that she has been betrayed, she fights as a man. She slashes Exum's face. When he strikes back, she faints. Her mock symptoms of pregnancy combined with a masculine-like attack quantify the force of Cassie Lee's maternal desire.

Cassie Lee's protest announces her movement toward self-definition as she distinguishes the power of God from the authority of man. Wearing a cowrie cross around her neck that symbolizes an African-centered interpretation of Christianity, she incorporates the female in the Christianizing process. Central to Cassie Lee's concept of Christianity is that the female should have a self-determined moral conscience. Her decision to live outdoors as a free woman rather than indoors as Exum's prostitute underscores her belief. Living outdoors in cardboard boxes and eating discarded food takes a toll on her body after Exum puts her out in the snow, but her soul is free. In celebrating moral goodness, she deflates the ego of the parasitic male.

Cassie Lee's continued growth toward self-definition and self-esteem also has class implications. Refusing to have sex with undeserving men, she elevates herself above the status of a slave woman. Even Exum Taylor views her as a woman with class. Of all the women that Exum Taylor has pleasured, Cassie Lee is the only one to reject him. She peddles eggs and vegetables and washes laundry rather than accepts his illicit offers. Generating Exum's dislike for her, she also gains his respect because he knows she respects herself. Cassie Lee's pride in herself includes her desire to be home centered. Unable to establish a home with Exum, she sets as her goal to become a boardinghouse owner and establish family-like relations with boarders whom she can assist.

Cassie Lee's effectiveness in defining herself is underscored in her romantic relationship with Solomon Hawk. Although she loves Solomon Hawk, rumors of his cheating on her with the prostitute Ming make her more determined than ever not to be sexually used by a man. The value she places on herself is rooted in both the Christian ethic of faithfulness and her own definition of gender freedom. Not knowing for sure whether Solomon Hawk has transgressed, she maintains her pride when he tells her to leave his home to pursue her dream of obtaining a boardinghouse. His ultimatum is beneficial to her, not malicious. In less than a year, she is forced to engage in a third search for a home.

Race, gender, and class become interweaving components at Bohemia's brothel, where Cassie Lee secures a job as cook. Race comes to figure in the presence of the Fugitive Slave Law, which could remand Cassie Lee to slavery. As an ex-slave, Cassie Lee protests the political injustice of the law by correcting her mannerisms that manifest her slave past and by isolating certain habits as a means of projecting a new image. To manifest the confidence that goes with being a free person, she buys a gun, practices shooting it, learns to read, and saves $150 for her passage from Sacramento to San Francisco.

Secure as a cook at Bohemia's brothel, Cassie Lee is caught up in the race/gender/class stigma attached to black women who are unable to find jobs other than as whores. Cassie Lee protests being considered as having low repute simply because she works at the brothel. She stands up to Lucas Davenport, the father of Samuel, the eleven-year-old who sells her eggs, because he associates all the women working at the brothel as whores. Her confrontation with Lucas makes clear her disapproval of his racist and patriarchal assessment of black women and class. To Cassie Lee, Davenport's conception of class discriminates against her as a black woman simply because she works at the brothel. In Cassie Lee's mind, character is based on a person's behavior, values, and ethics, not her association with others. As a dirt farmer, who cannot tell Cassie Lee to her face what he thinks about her, Davenport misses the mark of decency, according to Cassie Lee.

As Cassie Lee grows in her mock maternity, she expands her beneficence. Her giving can be contrasted to the selfishness of Bohemia, her employer. Cassie Lee feeds a twelve-year-old homeless girl that Bohemia turns away. An ambiguous woman who gauges her monetary progress by her hard work, Bohemia believes in the survival of the fittest. Bohemia's character is linked to the selfish notion that charity breeds poverty and to her own flawed relationship with her class-biased family. In contrast to Bohemia's taking, Cassie Lee gives. Overwhelmed by the child's neediness, Cassie Lee feeds her, thinks about clothes to offer her, and then wonders what will happen to the child. The extent of Cassie Lee's philanthropic concern manifests her conviction that black children would never go hungry if she were as rich as Bohemia.

In motherhood, the refiguration stage, Cassie Lee gives birth to herself as an abolitionist and community uplift worker. With a successful boardinghouse and money from Bohemia and Exum, she backs runaway slaves and offers young blacks employment. Her abolitionist ventures stem as much from her benevolence as they do from her deep satisfaction in helping others to realize their freedom. With no family of her own, she functions as a maternal agent for young fugitives and for Juanita, alias Candy, one of Bohemia's former prostitutes. Cassie Lee underscores her belief in others' worthiness in the motherly advice she gives to Juanita: Cassie Lee makes clear that she thinks Juanita is a decent woman who can contribute to the uplift of the community and should not waste her time with men who cannot forget about her past as a prostitute.

The advice that Cassie Lee gives to Juanita is the guidance that she governs her own life by. It is the same intelligence that Solomon Hawk uses in searching for and finding Cassie Lee, who still loves him and whom he discovers he is unable to live without. A risk taker and believer in the goodness of humankind, Cassie Lee sells her property and moves to a Napa Valley ranch called Destiny that Hawk has purchased. Secure in her new home, Cassie Lee realizes her full maternity. She cares for orphans left on her doorstep and gives birth to her own daughter, whom she names Miracle Destiny. Her success in her marriage to Solomon derives from her ability to combine strengths that transcend gender with a benevolence that distinguishes her as a maternal figure.

Beverly Jenkins's *Indigo*

The leguminous plant indigo and the deep, rich, dark blue permanent dye obtained from its leaves and stems had given rise to an indigo culture that was firmly established in the southern United States by the eighteenth century; the plant furnished the blue dye for the Continental uniform.[39] It is the namesake of Jenkins's 1996 novel *Indigo*, which, compared with *Nowhere to Run*, has more emphasis on the freedom struggle. It vividly dramatizes the abolitionist movement as the historic setting which called black women to action. Set in Whittaker, Michigan, in 1858, the novel introduces a year in the critical second phase of the movement—a time calling for immediate rather than gradual freedom for black people. The North became the flight destination of fugitive slaves, many of whom were welcomed by free black women who had themselves at one time been slaves. The life of the legendary antislavery agent Harriet Tubman[40] is the model of black female resistance by which the character of twenty-two-year-old Hester Wyatt, abolitionist agent, is revealed.

In *Indigo*, the character development appropriately starts *in medias res* (in the middle of the sequence of events), moves backward in time, and terminates open ended. This unconventional, nineteenth-century structure allows for the black woman's nontraditional telling of her story, which has been traditionally told from the perspective of the white male. Within this unconventional structure is a parallel structure of maternal importance involving the protagonist's growth via insemination, gestation, and birth. The superimposed maternal text appropriately complements the black woman abolitionist's involvement in a predominantly male movement.

Hester Wyatt's mock insemination occurs when she is a child. Her abolitionist aunt, acting on directions from Hester's father, ships Hester north to Detroit via the Underground Railroad. Hester's migration owing to a male-inspired copula thrusts her into a movement that depends on the African-based helping tradition for its support. Sheltering fugitive slaves who arrive at her Detroit home reveals Hester as a defiant character working for the good of her race. She is consciously motivated by the discrepancy between what slavery has denied her and her family and what she desires for her people.

The narrative commences at a critical point (*in medias res,* gestation) in the career of Hester Wyatt, to whose Detroit home is brought a slave family along with the wounded Black Daniel, the most feared and notorious antislavery agent on the circuit. Hester's decision to care for the Black Daniel, whom she discovers is Galen Vashon, a wealthy Louisiana resident, illuminates her deep involvement in the movement. Working for an order that originated with successful black male Underground Railroad conductors, Hester houses runaway slaves in the passageways of the large Michigan home bequeathed to her by her abolitionist aunt, and she belongs to the Detroit Ladies Abolition Circle. She supports the Free Produce Movement, refusing to buy goods such as cotton, rice, and sugar produced by slaves, and a black vigilante group modeled after the New York Committee of Vigilance, which David Ruggles, a black man, founded in 1835. Through her work, Hester becomes the fictional representative of black antislavery agents who commenced what Henrietta Buckmaster refers to as a "'crusade of the conscience' that rested upon a separate parallel institutional and organizational infrastructure of struggle and resistance."[41]

During the freedom struggle, Hester experiences gestational pangs of racism. Her most formidable foe is Ezra Shoe, a rapacious white slave owner who searches her home for Galen and threatens to remand Hester to slavery if Galen is caught in her home. As a perceptive, well-organized activist, Hester plans ahead for Shoe's visit and uses trickery to mask her subversive actions. Pretending to entertain a sewing club when she is hosting a local gathering of female abolitionists, Hester conceals a revolver in her lap under sewing material and wears gloves to hide her indigo-stained hands. Shoe's evil is metaphorically represented in his smelly, unwashed body, which nauseates Hester and causes her hands to shake. Hester has significant reason to react to Shoe's presence. She bears the marks that, if discovered, could return her to slavery. As a child laborer on an indigo plantation in South Carolina,[42] her hands and feet were permanently stained by blue dye. A trope of disfigurement reinforcing the theme of racial dehumanization, indigo dye is the identifying factor that could return Hester, now a free woman who wears white gloves, to slavery. She fears that indigo dye on her hands will forever brand her a slave.

As a free yet "branded" black woman, Hester struggles against the double threats based in race and gender. Her race exposes her to exploitation and ultimately determines her gender poverty; she is a product of the racialized history that has always regarded black women as sexually available. Menaced by Shoe and his bounty hunters, who attempt to gang-rape her and remand her to slavery, Hester holds them at bay with a revolver and debunks the myth of the constitutionally "lascivious" black woman. To Hester's thinking, white men actually believed that black women wanted them sexually. Hester's refusal to submit to forced sex locates her gender identity and her character on a higher plane, one based on choice and desire, qualities attributed to human emotions, not bestial appetite. She embodies the African American woman's perspective on an issue seldom realized in histories that others write about her.

Gender bias also emanates from Galen Vashon, who hinders Hester's effectiveness as a caregiver. Despite Hester's warnings, Galen insists on proceeding with his abolitionist endeavors before his healing is complete. His bad mood, gruff tone, and refusal to take orders clearly manifest his masculine assertiveness over Hester even when he needs her most. Asserting that Hester's ointment smells like a woman, he forces a distinction in the work that black men and black women perform for the abolitionist cause. They confer briefly as equals about the community's traitor who has informed Shoe of Galen's whereabouts, but Galen clearly represents the "strong" black male who regards his public role as more important than Hester's. Counteracting Galen's impatience, Hester, who considers him the crudest man she has ever met, relies on patience and time to settle their differences.

As patriarchy becomes romance, Hester embodies an internal conflict between asceticism and sensuality. By day, she keeps her body covered, giving the promiscuous Galen the impression that she is not a worldly woman. At night, she dons a sensuous, green silk gown whose lacy edging barely covers her breasts. The open, green dress that Galen has sent her metaphorically represents the budding, fertile essence of Hester's maturity. Looking in the mirror at herself, Hester does not recognize herself. Feeling sexy, she removes her coarse underwear to better feel the delicate silk hug her waist and hips. Hester's emerging sensuality speaks to her developing gender liberation. However, until she finds love, Hester minimizes her allure, even though Galen is attracted to her.

Romance buds, and Hester is exposed to class prejudice. Busybodies label her a "whore" as she visits Galen's home to consummate their relationship. The distinction between "whore" and "lady" often resides in a community's acceptance or rejection of woman's work. The two roles are mutually exclusive in the Christian community that Hester lives in and leave no room for blending. While Hester's work as an abolitionist is honorable, her fornication is not. Yet, Hester's participation in lovemaking with Galen seals a caring relationship and upsets the distinction of lady/whore and good/evil. Their bond energizes a chivalric sentiment in Galen, who eloquently defends Hester in church against the town's gossip. Her respectability is reinstated when Galen informs the church that he wants Hester as his wife, not his whore.

As Galen's wife, Hester's presence in his family intersects class prejudice and exposes Hester for the first time to intraracial prejudice. As a dark-complexioned ex-slave with indigo-stained hands, she belongs to a class outside the Louisiana Creoles, or *gens de coleur libres*, that Galen's family and friends represent. Her social position is historically rooted in an eighteenth-century practice that began when Spain assumed control over Louisiana, which subsequently began a census to distinguish between freeborn and slaveborn blacks and between light-skinned blacks (*pardos*) and the darker-hued (*morenos*).[43]

With her activist background of patience, love, and fortitude, Hester withstands the snobbish and frilly mannerisms of the *gens de coleur libres*. She stands up to the contemptuous female element that desires Galen, and her race love counterpoints the insidious race hatred of Galen's near-white grandmother Vada Vashon, who bought and sold slaves and even disowned her own daughter (Galen's mother) because she wedded a laborer with dark skin.[44] Hester's altruism contrasts Vada's selfishness. Not only does Hester raise funds to help others, but she harbors no class prejudice when aiding the light-complexioned Ellen Craft and her darker-hued husband, William, in their escape to freedom. Hester's benevolence as Underground Railroad conductor is enfolded in a tradition that allows her greater insight into the human condition and an identification with a cause greater than herself. Manifesting love in her work, Hester sustains herself. Giving love, Hester is everything that Vada despises. Her morality, intelligence, and race love even distinguish Hester from the perfumed predatory beauties who pass themselves off as virgins and are Vada's light-complexioned friends, Hester's competitors, and Galen's discards.

The race/gender/class weight that Hester bears as an abolitionist results in a delayed birth of freedom (the novel closes open ended). This unfinished ending reminds the reader of the work that still needed to be done for slavery's closure, despite Hester's personal triumphs, and it signals the impracticality of a final stasis. Hester's ruminations on this issue reflect her continued deep feelings about her activist mission. As a married woman, Hester has a good husband, has found her mother, and is pregnant with her first child. Despite this good fortune, she believes that only the end of slavery can make her life complete. The novel's quasi-celebratory ending confirms Hester's hope of a better future as she looks forward to slavery's end and the birth of her child. These events will complete her own maturation.

Hester, Cassie Lee, and Emily appear in plots with a maternal thread, yet their resistance to America's oppression is gendered male. They don't just migrate; they take lengthy journeys to foreign lands—Detroit, the Sierra Nevada, and Texas. Employing male tactics, they gain leverage through trickery, quasi-military maneuvers, and physical force. Hester and Cassie Lee carry guns for protection, and all three heroines manifest the strength of soldiers in combat. Their preparations for race, gender, and class battles follow the mandate of Maria W. Stewart, who argued for the "spirit of men," bold and courageous, as an important formula for black women's self-empowerment. These strong heroines expand the range of mulattas in nineteenth-century fiction who were decidedly feminine, distanced from brothels, and always unarmed in a crisis.

2 Civil War Volunteerism

The Call to Reconstitute Family

Sable Fontaine in Beverly Jenkins's *Through the Storm*

As the Civil War ruptured black slave kinship groups, black women volunteered to reconstruct the family. Their volunteerism had its history in American slavery, under which the black family had contracted and expanded according to the economic constrictions of plantation life. From the two-parent patriarchal unit,[1] to the mother/child dyad, to different configurations of kin across generations, and to the extended family with nonrelational kin,[2] the survival of the kinship group depended on its flexibility, its adaptive strategy. Darlene Clark Hine writes, "The black response to an institution that tore families apart in the name of economics was to improvise other families."[3] *Other families* most often included a black female—a sister, grandmother, or surrogate mother who assumed responsibility for the care of the children on the plantation. This female became the constitutive and protective agent for the innocent in a race-biased environment, no matter how tenuous her gender role or demeaning her class status.

Race difference meant race self-sufficiency during slavery's demise. War-related impressments, conscription, and relocation exacerbated the separation of black families that slavery started and made it necessary for black women to maintain their own families. They were left without provisions when slave owners refused to provide for them and their children after black men absented themselves to go to war on the Union side,[4] and women who rushed with their children to already crowded Union camps were not well received. Their presence was regarded as a hindrance to the male's military efficiency, and they were forced to leave the camp. According to Bardaglio, "At Camp Nelson, Kentucky, white soldiers evicted hundreds of [black] women and children in November 1864, leaving them with no shelter from the bitterly cold weather."[5] If they were allowed to remain at the camps, the burden of dependent black women often proved to be too awesome for the Contraband Relief Commission and the Bureau of Refugees, Freedmen and Abandoned Lands, whose policy was that a free people, even without sufficient resources, should be self-managing.

Ironically, the same economic imperative that splintered slave families before the war resurfaced during and after the war to reconfigure kinship members under a patriarchal head. Reconstituting the black family into a two-parent unit seemed to have been the states' solution to the problem of so-called "black poverty." Historian Katherine M. Franke writes that the "state's recognition of the integrity of the African American family was motivated, in significant part, by a desire to privatize dependency. By installing the husband as the head and fiscal sovereign of his family, the state absolved itself of responsibility for the cost of care of needy *women* and children."[6] Franke's assessment of the situation proves the predicament black women found themselves in. They could not depend on the states for help, and many had no men to rely on.

The southern states' efforts to install a patriarchal head proved futile. Slavery and the war had made deep ruptures in the two-parent structure that defied immediate repair. Then, too, the South, in its efforts to raise revenue and reestablish itself, instituted vagrancy laws to incarcerate black men and established apprenticeship laws to indenture black children to whites. Incarceration and indentureship exacerbated the separation of black family members. In Louisiana, the setting for Beverly Jenkins's *Through the Storm* (1998), vagrancy and apprenticeship laws were established as early as October 1865 in local parishes. The incarceration of black men and the kidnapping of black children sounded the call for black women to reconstitute black families. Their work became even more necessary when thousands of black orphans roamed the streets after the state's apprenticeship program replaced black orphanages and group homes that the government had supported. "Othermothers," a term I borrow from Patricia Hill Collins,[7] came to the rescue of defenseless children whose parents were lost, kidnapped, remanded to slavery, or dead.

The disadvantages of race presented gender and class challenges. Nineteenth-century black women, therefore, politicized the disruption of black families. They wrote themselves into a white patriarchal history that absolved itself of any duty to ease black families into freedom and that too often looked upon blacks at emancipation as irresponsibly dependent, promiscuous, and vile. With the absence of black men, black women bore the gender responsibility of caring for families even though they had little to provide. Charlotte Burris, a black woman testifying before the American Freedmen's Inquiry Commission in December 1863, took exception to how black women providers were stereotypically perceived. Burris declared, "We have never been dependent; we have never been troublesome to anybody. If it is little we have enough, and are satisfied with what we have."[8] Burris's words suggest a familial-type sharing in the black community that has its origins in an African-derived helping tradition.

Black women heeding the call to reconstitute and stabilize the black kinship group inherited a legacy of caring from their African female forebears. One of the various kinship models in which African women exhibited maternal humanism and strength was the matrifocal family. Prevalent in West African slave-trading countries such as Ghana and transported to American slaveholding states, the matrifocal family gave to the African woman true equality with the man. She made decisions, had a public presence, asserted her individuality, and demonstrated her concern for human welfare. Caring for herself and others proved her ability to hold the family together and demonstrate her independence. As Jeanne Noble asserts, "[The African woman] has always demonstrated strength and self-reliance—necessary qualities for survival. . . . Female equality is enough of a historical thread in the history of Africa for women *never* to have developed a concept of themselves as worthless or dependent."[9]

The tradition of black women stabilizing families has a history in African American literature from Harper to McMillan. The title character Iola Leroy in Harper's 1892 novel searches for and finds her missing mother; Janie's grandmother in Hurston's *Their Eyes Were Watching God* takes Janie in and cares for her after the death of her own daughter; and Mildred Peacock in McMillan's *Mama* rears five children in the absence of her errant husband. In these novels, female caregivers administer primarily to other females to protect them from tentacles of racism that lead to gender abuse and economic deprivation. The caregivers are supportive and responsible attendants, but the care given is to those of blood kin and is motivated by family obligation. The characters perform their tasks free from any duty to the community and independent of an acknowledged attachment to an African helping tradition. Beverly Jenkins's *Through the Storm* expands on these latter issues. The novel locates the care given by Sable Fontaine, the heroine, to family members and to nonrelational kin. She works within the helping tradition, which manifests her duty to others and her desire to uplift the community. Her caregiving is instructive. She educates others to care for themselves. The results of her care become more important than the racism that produced a need for her assistance.

Through the Storm dramatizes the transference of the African-based female helping tradition in the confluence of relationships that Sable Fontaine is exposed to. An archetypal caregiver in African American literature, Sable is the conduit through which the elements of the African helping tradition are received and passed on. Born a slave, she is a descendant of a matrilineal line of royal African queens, the last of whom, her Aunt Mahti, cared for her as a child and then prepared for her care by others. Sable repeats the cycle of helping others by assuming custodianship of others' children. Sable's character is revealed through what other characters say about her and through her actions. These revelations unveil a laddered strengthening of her character as she evolves from a dependent, literate house slave to an independent Civil War volunteer and community worker. Like the heroines discussed in chapter 1, her growth is measured in a maternally designed narrative that charts the stages of virginity, gestation, and motherhood.

The twenty-nine-year-old, green-eyed Sable comes to life in a saga whose freedom-conscious narrator draws attention to the aesthetic and economic decline of the southern white slavocracy and the rise of the virginal Sable. The description of the Fontaine mansion that once required the labor of fifteen slaves *just to maintain its lawns* is now run-down and nearly deserted. This mansion sets the necessary stage for Sable's growth as the South wanes. This house is where Sable's female relatives were forced to breed but avenged themselves and where Sable defies Henry Morse, an illegal trafficker in slaves who intends to use her body for the same purpose. Valuing her maidenhead and expected freedom, Sable lets go of the emotions she has masked and warns her prospective owner that despite all of his money, he is still trash to her. In speaking, Sable writes herself into the political arena and demonstrates one of the few means of strength that the female slave had access to—her voice. She opposes what Henry Morse represents: a defiler of black families, a dehumanizer of black flesh for capital gain, and a seeker of pleasure for pleasure's sake. Her voice identifies her impertinence and confidence—necessary qualities for resistance. She desires a better life for herself and recognizes the relationship between voice and empowerment even as Morse threatens her. The voice/empowerment relationship, says feminist scholar Luce Irigaray, implies that one who finds a voice can find a way.[10]

Sable finds a way to freedom. Her first journey from slave house to contraband relief camp begins with the authoritative voice of her dying Aunt Mahti, an African matriarch who awakens Sable's consciousness to a legacy of familial bonding and beneficence. With Mahti's kind words and her gift of an old canvas bag, Sable is initiated into the family-based African helping tradition. Each time that Sable removes items from the bag, she primes her character as a person of beneficence. From the bag, Sable takes a yam to stave off her hunger, a skin of water to quench her thirst, and a gold bracelet to link her to her African roots. The food and drink represent a celebration of the construction of Sable's maturing self; they compose the feast traditionally regarded, in Patricia Yaeger's words, as "a time of empowerment."[11] The celestial patterns on the gold bracelet match those that Aunt Mahti carved on Sable's upper thigh at Sable's puberty. As symbolic representations, the celestial configurations on Sable's body and bracelet record a survival legacy that Aunt Mahti passes on to her. Together, these carvings reveal that in the tradition of Aunt Mahti's African village, scarring and an offering (the bracelet) compose the initiation rite into womanhood.

As in Jenkins's *Indigo,* the figure of Harriet Tubman again figures prominently, this time in the flesh—as the surrogate mother and masculinized copula who induces Sable's vicarious gestation as a woman. In *Through the Storm,* Tubman is called by her actual birth name, Araminta. She fills Sable with food and shelters her en route to the contraband camp. This female giving advances the plot of the character development and moves beyond the caregiving for blood kin traditionally found in African American women's novels. Araminta's assistance endows Sable with thoughtfulness, politeness, and moral obligation as she learns the importance of giving and becomes aware of the sacrifices the giver often has to make. Her bonding with Araminta underscores the successful transference of the black female helping tradition from black Africa, which Aunt Mahti represents, to black America, which Araminta manifests and passes on to Sable. The nonrelational kinship between Sable and Araminta makes Sable more cognizant of her similarity to Araminta, who relates how at seven years old, she fled from the plantation but returned because of hunger.

Sable's insemination with the female helping tradition leads to a mock first trimester; in reality, she is kept safe from gender abuse and class demoralization through Araminta's caregiving. Eating an initiation meal of hardtack dipped in coffee prior to entering the contraband camp, Sable braves her first gestational upset. She refuses to join young black women in the camp who prostitute their bodies to white officers. Instead, she takes a job for ten cents a day, washing clothes in a tub containing lye and hot water. Her job choice illuminates her moral integrity and marks her humbleness despite the inconvenience of red, chapped hands. Sable's bone-paining work becomes her way of celebrating her maternal ancestors and bringing significance to her own life.

In a gestational trope, Sable extends herself by embracing the African folk tradition of communal sharing. In two specific instances during her first week in camp, Sable volunteers her time to aid displaced fugitives and rebuild nonrelational families. In the first instance, she stops her paid work to help Patrick, a lost child in the camp, to find his uncle, his only surviving relative. Her commitment to Patrick overrides everything. She is determined to move heaven and earth to reunite Patrick and his relative. Assuming responsibility for Patrick,

Sable acknowledges her obligation to protect the black child in the family-shattered fugitive slave community. Protecting Patrick echoes her Aunt Mahti's protection of her on the plantation after the passing of her mother. This protection extends the female caregiver-receiver relationship in black literature to female caregiver and male-receiver relationships. As fictive kin, Sable transfers the black woman's obligation to care for all children from the slave plantation to the Union contraband camp.

In the second instance, Sable expands the family circle to include the distraught and tearful Avery Coles. Asking the illiterate Coles if she can assist him in some way, Sable aids him by reading to him the message his literate wife has posted for him on the Message Tree. Reading to Avery Coles is more than a passing amusement; it is a means to reconnect physically separated loved ones. These instances with Coles and Patrick reveal Sable's offer to reconstitute the family in two of the more tragic outcomes of slavery—the separation of the black child from the primary caregiver and the deprivation of blacks' education. The calm that Sable exudes, despite various setbacks, suggests an expected imposition that black female almsgivers realized in the war-torn South.

Sable's good deeds appropriately complement the altruism of Raimond LeVeq, the black major at the contraband relief camp and romantic hero, to whom Araminta introduces Sable and who offers Sable and Patrick dinner in his camp. LeVeq's tasty meal consisting of chicken, collards, and yams functions as the preparatory feast that joins him and Sable in mutual benevolence. A freeborn Haitian reared in Louisiana and forever reminded of race difference, LeVeq has concerned himself with defending the black race in whatever way possible. He has joined the Union Army as a proud member of a black regiment, the First Louisiana Native Guard. As major, his job is to process the black refugees entering the camp, but he is moved by a moral consciousness to aid the contraband after realizing the enormity of their problems and understanding their inability to solve them. The similarity that LeVeq shares with Sable in helping the slave masses reveals the importance of Sable as a person in stabilizing the communal family in the face of racial injustice.

Race merges with gender as Sable is exposed to LeVeq's masculine interest and bias, to which she responds aggressively. On the one hand, she rejects LeVeq's interest in her by refusing his job offer of clerk and by disapproving of his special treatment of her at camp. And in another instance, she denies LeVeq's insinuation that she is sexually servicing Rhine, who LeVeq is unaware is Sable's brother. Intolerant of LeVeq's questioning of her character, Sable verbally flays him. She tells him that Rhine's money is as good as his and that he should find someone else to wash his clothes. Sable's resistance comes as LeVeq observes her poorly fitting dress, mud-caked shoes, dark, thick hair, prominent nose, and full mouth—descriptive signals that clearly identify Sable as one of the folk and that anchor her to an African folk tradition. What her outburst reveals is that despite her lower-class status, she does not want to accept help from LeVeq if it means lowering her character. Yet, when she sides with her brother, the family deserter who passes for white, rather than with LeVeq, who has aided her and is enamored with her, she manifests ambiguity. The complexity of her character can be explained by her sense of one's right to choose one's freedom and whether or not to give or accept help.

Sable's second journey (second trimester), from the contraband camp to her flight to the North, exposes her to less gender bias than in the first trimester. It begins with her desire for her own freedom and exposes her single indiscretion—theft. Motivated by fear of Henry Morse's entry into the camp and distrust of LeVeq's push for her to become his mistress, Sable pilfers LeVeq's gold and heads to the North. Sable's taking is not without giving; she leaves behind her gold bracelet to replace LeVeq's pilfered gold. Her unequal exchange reveals her sense of fairness in a state of dire need, but it leaves her guilt ridden and gives LeVeq considerable cause to doubt Sable's character. Even so, her decision to act manifests the importance of freedom that she inscribes for herself.

Sable prefers freedom over reenslavement and reveals that what she says about freedom reflects her true mind. She is determined not to return to slavery. Sable's decision is a practical one; her physical being must be free in order for her to help others. Her settlement in Boston baptizes her into a temporary freedom and bonds her to Verena Jackson, a near-blind elderly, ill widow, to whom Sable renders daughterly care. The Sable-Verena relationship exhibits yet another pattern of bonding and obligation between nonrelational youth and elderly seldom read about in African American women's literature. Insisting that the best health care should be given the stubborn Verena, Sable is rewarded. She inherits Verena's fortune. Caregiving between Sable and Verena thus becomes interchangeable, with each woman participating in the gender and class viability of the other.

Sable's journey north to Boston to her new home with Verena grants her a physical freedom from Henry Morse, but it alienates her from her past. Her separation from the South is more than a geographical rupture; it brings on deep emotional stress and a change of name from Sable (meaning to darken) to Elizabeth Clark (implicating "passing," and suggesting a play on the name Sappho Clark in Pauline Hopkins's *Contending Forces*). Sable's change of names expands on the passing theme prevalent in nineteenth-century historical novels. Her name change is temporary and is accompanied with bouts of sadness for family members and friends lost. The reader gathers that Sable regards the South as home and that in the South, to which she longs to return, she can reclaim her true identity and atone for her wrongdoing.

Sable's third journey (third trimester), to New Orleans, marks the period of her redemption and further growth. Her atonement is accomplished in the home of Juliana LeVeq, a communal caregiver, Raimond LeVeq's mother, and close friend of Verena Jackson, who returns to her hometown to die. In the security of Juliana's home, Elizabeth Clark unveils her true identity and the reason for her theft. Shedding her false name, Sable reclaims the name given to her by her African ancestors and thus reestablishes herself in the community of female African caregivers. Her successful transfiguration through her name change can be gathered in the response of Juliana, who never regarded the name "Elizabeth" as a proper one for Sable. Sable impresses Juliana as an unvarnished woman, one Juliana would like for a daughter-in-law. To Juliana, Sable is not an addle-brained woman who will waste her time shopping and visiting hairdressers. She is someone who will give to Raimond as much as he gives to her.

Sable is a younger version of the older Juliana LeVeq. Both women have a royal past that the war eroded. Both have lost family to the war. Both show their humility in the tattered clothes they wear and in their refusal to ask for help. And like Juliana, Sable's grief motivates her to help others. Magnifying the precariousness of black women's economic fate in the Civil War debacle, both women embody the concern for others' destinies that they mirror themselves.

Sable's atonement connects her to Juliana's financial ruin and to her own penalty for theft. Sable pays a heavy price in agreeing to marry Raimond, whose primary intent is to satisfy the stipulations of his mother's paternal grandfather's will, which requires him to take a wife and sire a child in order to reestablish Juliana's position of wealth. Sable braces herself for Raimond's impertinent announcement that once she carries his child, his duties as husband will end. She stands up to class bias from LeVeq's well-to-do friends, who tell her that she is not good enough to marry into the LeVeq family. Despite these setbacks, Sable empowers Juliana, who regains her wealth, and stabilizes herself in that family. As Raimond's wife, she and her children will be provided for; staying in the family would be a better life for Sable than trying to eke out an existence in the streets of New Orleans. This phase of Sable's social gestation produces a range of emotions, from anger to relief, but she maintains her faith in the strength of family. The degree of Sable's gender suffering manifests the extent to which southern states did, in fact, absolve themselves of the responsibility to mitigate black female poverty. Yet, in her suffering, Sable has the strength of mind and body to bring forth life.

As a new community mother, Sable dedicates herself to protecting homeless black waifs left on the streets by the deaths of their parents or by parents forced into a contract work system. She takes in and adopts three of eighteen illiterate, rat-bitten, lice-infected foundlings. She feeds, clothes, and beds them down and instructs one adolescent on the care of her menses. Removing black children from the streets of New Orleans, Sable lessens children's exposure to violence, crime, prostitution, and peonage. Committed to the stabilization of the black communal family and the care of black children, Sable becomes an archetypal othermother.

As othermother, Sable launches two careers. She constructs an orphanage and a schoolhouse, without which the living standard of black waifs would not improve. As orphanage proprietor and teacher, Sable responds to the government's failure to benefit thousands of black children left homeless in the transition from slavery to freedom. The orphanage was a cultural container alien to the traditional African in the nineteenth century, but Sable, as orphanage proprietor and family stabilizer, represents the link connecting the black helping tradition to the modern practice of institutionalized social work.

Sable's successful work as othermother complicates her pregnancy by her husband. The danger comes from Henry Morse, who believes that the emancipation of slaves was the worst thing that ever happened in the South. Dedicating his life to returning blacks to slavery, Morse shackles the pregnant Sable and her three adopted children and carries them to his plantation to plant a cotton crop. Sable's reexposure to the plantation replays race/gender/class biases that have combined to deconstruct the black family. Sable exhibits a spirituality in her ordeal and manifests the strength that has inspired her maternal ancestors: She sadly prays for strength to return home with her children. Central to Sable's spirituality is her affirmation of responsibility for others' well-being and a recognition of mourning as an acceptable expression of everyday black life. Her faith sees her through her ordeal with Henry Morse and the birth pangs of delivering her daughter, Desiree Mahti.

With Sable Fontaine, Beverly Jenkins brings to the historical romance genre an archetypal character functioning in several roles to reconstitute the black family. As community scribe, nurse, daughter, othermother, and mother, Sable proves her own worth and subverts the lie of the ubiquitous helpless, poverty-stricken black woman dependent on whites for sustenance in the war-torn South. Credibly sustaining the portrayal of the strong black woman, Sable expands depictions of black women characters presented in earlier historical romances. Her strength and perseverance contrast Iola Leroy's weakness and irresolution. Iola Leroy becomes ill, works in the shadow of her husband, and bears no children. She seeks direction from Dr. Latimer, but then doubts her capability to follow through on his suggestions. In contrast, Sable remains healthy, gives birth to a daughter, and intuitively knows what to do.

Sable, too, is the antithesis of Desiree Hippolyte, the quadroon who grooms herself to be taken care of for life by her white paramour in Frank

Yerby's *The Foxes of Harrow*. As mistress, Desiree causes Stephen Fox to hasten the death of his first wife, and she thrives in a narrative of family dissolution. Desiree is the catalyst of discord between Stephen and his son Etienne and between Etienne and his intended bride. Separated from her family and abandoned in her pregnancy by Stephen, Desiree lives without a link to the strong African tradition of communal sharing. Beverly Jenkins corrects the deficiencies in the portrayal of Yerby's Desiree by naming Sable's daughter Desiree Mahti and clearly positioning the child in a female tradition of sharing that was Aunt Mahti's, her maternal forebear's.

Through Sable's vigorous actions for family stability, *Through the Storm* offers a broader view of the black female caregiver in the historical romance genre and in black literature generally. The heroine's feats of strength and endurance reveal a willing worker for communal and familial togetherness. In her political assertiveness, Sable rescues indigent, lost, and disconnected black kinship groups. Her activism in a historical moment of blacks' dispossession reclaims a segment of black women's history that nineteenth-century romanticism and twentieth-century pulp fiction have omitted. By her own admission, Jenkins wanted to fill in the gaps where history said blacks did not exist.[12] She does just that with Sable Fontaine's commitment to restoring black families.

3 Postbellum Activism

The Call to Heal

Francine Craft's Katherine Keyes and Beverly Jenkins's Dr. Lancaster

Black women's call to heal following the Civil War is situated in America's nineteenth-century reform movement. Changes under way in the medical field were coterminous with temperance calls against alcohol and tobacco and with women's advocating for their rights. "Rational medicine," including diagnosis and clinical observation, gradually replaced bloodletting, purging, and blistering. Physicians subscribing to polypharmacy, the prescribing of multiple doses of different medicines for treatment or cure, vied with Thomsonians,[1] Eclectics,[2] homeopaths,[3] and hydropaths.[4] Alternative medical schools (homeopathic and Eclectic) opened their doors to women, and the gradual replacement of the midwife by the physician gave rise to women's medical schools. Black women became activists in this reform movement as healers and trained medical practitioners.

Two ways in which black women participated in the medical reform movement can be documented. First, black women healed with the knowledge of roots and medicinal potions and cured illnesses when a white physician would or could not do so. Moreover, these same women often provided itinerant white male physicians with knowledge of herbal practices. One physician,

Dr. Francis Peyre Porcher (1824–1895), used the information provided by black women and later codified it into a useful medical botany after the Civil War.[5] Second, black women physicians, formally trained in American medical schools as professional midwives and specialists in women's diseases, revolutionized the medical field by assuming positions as physicians in a profession predominantly male and traditionally white. They competed with male physicians who had limited knowledge of women's illnesses and cared even less about the health of blacks. Although few in number,[6] black women doctors by the end of the nineteenth century had founded hospitals, social services agencies, and training schools for nurses.[7] These physicians, together with black folk healers, composed a dual system of health care in the black community.

Healers, nonmedical and medical, have been a staple in black fiction since the nineteenth century. Regarded as a familiar component in the black community, they have appeared as conjurers, prophets, root workers, spiritualists, midwives, and nurses. In black women's fiction, one recalls Iola, the nurse in Harper's *Iola Leroy* (1892); Madam Frances, the seeress in Hopkins's *Contending Forces* (1900); Prophet David in Ann Petry's *The Street* (1946); Soaphead Church, spiritualist, in Toni Morrison's *The Bluest Eye* (1970); Minnie Ransom, faith healer, in Toni Cade Bambara's *The Salt Eaters* (1980); and Sapphira, midwife and nurse, and Mama Day, conjurer, in Gloria Naylor's *Mama Day* (1993). What these characters have in common is the brief duration in which they actually engage in the healing arts. Either they are protagonists whose healing is secondary to the plot's action or they are minor characters whose brief actions hasten the fate of a primary character. As healers, they do not address the issue of a healing belief, and their healing, though consequential, seems either removed from any competitive forces in the healing practice or unrelated to any desired liberation from an oppressive race-biased environment. Often these healers are perceived as quick-fix agents in times of crisis.

Francine Craft's *The Black Pearl* (1996) and Beverly Jenkins's *Vivid* (1995) expand the portrayal and perception of healers presented in prior black women's fiction. These two historical romances center in nineteenth-century black women health professionals whose participation in and commitment and philosophical approach to the healing process form the basis of the narratives. Craft's Katherine Keyes and Jenkins's Dr. Viveca Lancaster befriend their patients as they contend with professional competition and oppressive societal forces. Refusing to sublimate desire to oppression, they substitute their own authority in the form of a militarized healing process because authority in itself fails to fulfill their personal and professional needs. The vigorous struggles of these two women leave the reader with a more humane and modern portrait of the black female health care professional. More realistic than stereotypic,

Katherine Keyes and Dr. Lancaster mature in a female helping tradition and work toward the good of the community. Since their resistance to authority brings positive rewards to their communities, a discourse of black womanist activism is realized.

Together, the two narratives inscribe two different militant healers in the same social history. *The Black Pearl* illuminates the life of Katherine Keyes, an ex-slave herbalist and midwife, from 1869 to1870 in New Orleans, where she challenges the racism of an ex–slave owner, sexism in her professional duties, and classism from a class-struck Caribbean herbalist. *Vivid* highlights Dr. Viveca Lancaster, a first-generation black woman physician, who resists race, gender, and class biases in 1876 in a rural northern black community where her competitor is an itinerant white male physician who bleeds his patients. Working during America's medical reform movement but disconnected from its mainstream because they are black women, both protagonists authorize their medical professions as self-help agencies. Effective in their professions, they do not lose a patient or bring bad results.

Francine Craft's Katherine Keyes in *The Black Pearl*

Katherine Keyes, the clairvoyant twenty-year-old herbalist heroine in *The Black Pearl*, figures in a character plot in which she appears to accommodate agents of authority when she actually militarizes her position in the community. Her seemingly contradictory actions reside in her inner drive for self-sufficiency and communal uplift. Going along with authority masks her resistance to it, while providing an avenue for self-positioning. Divine intervention aids her strategy. Born with a caul over her face, she is gifted with a second sight, enabling her to prefigure situations. She uses this intelligence to produce liberating circumstances. In three distinct situations, Katherine replaces the authority of oppressive social forces with the supremacy of her medicinal knowledge, and each instance uncovers a deeper level of her character.

In the first situation, Katherine is introduced as a woman of action in her relationship to her ex–slave master, Theodore Keyes, an absent character in the novel. She demonstrates her deep desire for self-sufficiency even though Keyes's absence highlights the racism that gives power to one group to harness the talents of another. Katherine's seemingly accommodative stance in remaining on the Bayou Plantation with her former master after freedom actually masks her motive to be near the roots and herbs in the forests that she and her frail grandfather know best and need for survival. She employs these roots in the novel's initial scene, where she wearily nurses back to health her grandfather stricken with yellow fever. Her effective medicinal applications allow her to dismiss the authority of racism inherent in Keyes's retaining his ex-slaves. She supplants this authority with the superior authority of herbal knowledge.

Race merges with gender and complicates Katherine's desires to sever patriarchal relations on the plantation and function in a loving romantic relationship prefigured in her dreams about a black prince. Gender is used as an exploited entity and is metaphorically defined in Katherine's mock rape by three white men, who, under the orders of Paul DeBeau, a white Creole ship captain, kidnap her as a substitute for her ailing grandfather, a renowned herbalist. The male copula, represented by her kidnappers, transfers her from desire to reality. Katherine's black prince sailing on the same ship, the *Robber Baron,* eventually liberates her through marriage, but also contributes to her sociohistorical stress. Her rupture from familiar environs to be transported to New Orleans by the Robber Baron ship is a modern trope on the forced transference of the African medical agent from Africa to America by slave ship. As a woman, Katherine is regarded as easy prey by her white captors, who, similar to slave master Keyes, want to control her herbalist powers.

Katherine's gender becomes the source of her stress and strength in DeBeau's home. She is expected to cure Guy DeBeau, Paul DeBeau's dying son, whose illness has been beyond the comprehension of any physician, while she fends off sexist remarks about her gender assertiveness in her prognosis. Her resistance to sexism takes the form of professional restraint. This strategy cloaks her feelings about male ignorance and allows her to diagnose destructive human repression in her patient, who subordinates himself to his domineering father. Katherine's strategy reveals the growing fortitude of a woman activist who prioritizes her medical career.

Katherine's restraint finds expression in the structuring of her character function. Focused and effective, she replaces the blundering, ineffective American physician, Dr. Francois St. Cyr. She blooms in her profession despite the discomforts of sociohistorical biases and the limitations of American medicine. She works in the 1860s, when France, not America, was regarded as the intellectual site of modern medicine. In this historic period, intellectuals, including Americans, assumed that those who had studied medicine in France were superior to the American physicians who were apprenticed but had no training in botany, pathology, "and some other subjects considered essential to a medical education abroad."[8] Katherine's replacement of Dr. St. Cyr in the DeBeau home indicates the ineffectiveness of nineteenth-century American medicine and the rise of the black woman herbalist in Louisiana. Katherine examines her patient and diagnoses his illness. She is ahead of her American contemporaries who failed to apply diagnosis and clinical observation, a failure which, in reality, resulted in many American physicians taking additional courses in France to learn "the use of the stethoscope, the art of diagnosis."[9]

Katherine's healing philosophy, rooted in ancient Kemetic medical practices, engages an African-centered approach conceptualizing what Katherine Bankole refers to elsewhere as an "African Living Belief System"—a way of

African life, a belief system that engages all of the senses "in a celebration of existence and the promulgation of the ancient Kemetic concept of Ma'at."[10] Named after the Egyptian goddess Ma'at,[11] who personifies justice and universal harmony, Ma'at as belief system embraces the virtues of "truth, justice, balance, righteousness, harmony, and reciprocity."[12] To achieve these standards, one must, as Katherine Keyes does, engage specific concepts and their complementary components in the African Living Belief System. One of the eight concepts in the African Living Belief System that Katherine uses is "Tools," the components of which include "fire, water, earth, herbs, implements, food, colors, vegetation."[13] Katherine vigorously dispenses water, herbs, food, and vegetation as healing agents to achieve a healing balance. This balance comes with her conscious medical purpose and her dedication to celebrate life.

Using the African Living Belief System, Katherine subscribes to a holistic approach to healing. She assesses the body, mind, and spirit. Based on a thorough investigation, combining observation and consultation with prior cases she has attended, she diagnoses Guy DeBeau's problem. She concludes that his debauched body conceals an internal repression resulting from the death of a girl he loved but his father did not approve of. Confirming this knowledge, Katherine bathes him internally and externally, a practice common among blacks, not whites, before the rise of hydropathy in America.[14] Her therapy includes a salt-glow bath containing brittle sea salt, followed by a yarrow tea bath. Utilizing additional herbs of red clover, nettle, hyssop, and lobelia to brew teas, she heals her patient.[15] Her applications evidence the value she places on the worth of the total person. Disregarding the race and gender of others, she dispenses health, without giving attention to her own "place" as a black female health provider. Her attitude allows her to carve out her own space as a *black female* healer in the home of DeBeau, who expects healing results but fails to understand the healing application.

Katherine's Afrocentric approach to healing emphasizes not only the parochial nature of American physicians but also the limitations of American medicine. American medicine defined itself by three specific criteria: 1) Remedies were effective for specific maladies, 2) Prior reliability determined the success of each remedy, and 3) All doctors could obtain the same result given the identical illness.[16] Based on these criteria, any illness or disease that could not be defined often went unnoticed, and patients whose physical ailments were precipitated by unknown causal factors simply went untreated. Medical procedures for treating illnesses suggest the defensive, protracted, and inhumane nature of American medicine. Rising above the limited medical practices of her time, Katherine takes an offensive, abbreviated, and humane approach to treating illnesses.

As herbalist, Katherine is predisposed to additional gender prejudice that eventually links her to class bias. Her capture under DeBeau's orders forces her hasty marriage to Martin Dominguez for protection on the *Robber Baron* and emphasizes her predicament as a black female in a patriarchal world. Agreeing to marry Martin for her own safety, Katherine engages in defensive bonding.[17] She marries as an act of resistance against a possible rape by white ruffians on ship and provides the reader another glimpse at how she manages her life in order to survive. While the marriage prevents an assault on her body by white sailors, it ironically denies the conjugal consummation between husband and wife. Katherine's expressive sexuality is misinterpreted as fear by her new husband, who delays consummation indefinitely. Unintentionally, she employs sexuality as a weapon to keep at bay a husband who incorrectly reads her demonstration of love.

In her marriage, Katherine encounters a third authoritarian situation in the form of classism. Her foil is Celie Dominguez, her sister-in-law, a Caribbean herbalist and former sweetheart of Martin Dominguez, whom she jilted to marry his brother, Raoul, now deceased. The essence of the class conflict between Celie and Katherine is birth status and complexion. Born free and light enough to pass for white, Celie lauds her status and color over Katherine, a nutmeg-complexioned ex-slave whom she refuses to shake hands with. Rejecting an expressive folk gesture of welcome and signifying on Katherine as an ignorant former slave woman, Celie informs the reader of her racialized ideology of class that denies her own slave heritage and familial relations. According to Celie's belief system, one born a slave could not possibly possess "class" because "class" is rooted in the authority of color that derives from race difference.

Class conflict is used as a manipulative device to illuminate the opposing motivations of two women seeking power in New Orleans, the site of resettlement for both. A natural counterpoint to Celie, Katherine serves the community, whereas Celie serves herself. A capitalist at heart, Celie aims to improve her economic index through a merger (marriage) to Martin, Katherine's husband. She orders Martin to marry her and think of the wealth they could have together. If Celie were to accomplish the merger by marrying Martin, a prosperous smith of beautiful ironwork, it would be the attainment of a goal representing what Nancy Hartsock calls "the materially defining feature of the capitalist."[18] Celie's attempt to displace Katherine affirms her "I"-centered character and validates her adherence to a Eurocentric pecking order based on birth affiliation and color superiority.

In contrast to Celie's individualist imperative, Katherine aids others. She gives rather than takes, and money is not an issue with her. Her work crosses race, gender, and class boundaries, as is evident in her delivering the baby of the governor's wife, who feels uncomfortable talking to a male physician about the birthing process. Katherine is a thoughtful, caring, good person. She succeeds as a medical professional because she respects her patients.

Katherine's and Celie's opposing motivations illuminate their contrasting emotions and their primary differences as characters. Celie thrives on hatred and jealousy, Katherine on love and trust. Celie violates the Kemetic principle of "feeling" associated with communal unity; Katherine embodies that unity. Katherine operates on the complementary Kemetic concepts of "sound" (the oral medical instructions that she gives to her patients) and "feeling" (spiritual harmony). She wants her patient to think and feel what she says. The harmonious interaction between the oral and the kinetic provides the mental, physical, and spiritual synergy necessary for Katherine's creative and curative processes. Her empathy humanizes the relationship between healer and patient and reveals the trust and caring involved. Her patient/healer relationship is instructive because even Dr. St. Cyr receives an education from her.

Education, or at least its application, further distinguishes Katherine and Celie as characters and links their natural emotions to the attribution of cultural knowledge. Katherine utilizes cultural knowledge inherent in the African Living Belief System. To root out objectionable elements leading to physical, mental, and spiritual decline, for instance, she cleanses her patients. Her action prioritizes the restoration of health and spirituality and validates the cultural center of her people. Celie, in contrast, abuses the African Living Belief System through her misapplication of Voodoo, a derivative of the system.[19] Approaching Voodoo[20] from the Eurocentric perspective, as a primitive evil ritual, rather than from an African worldview, Celie feels herself above practicing the rite. Instead, she hires Dahomey Sinclair, a Voodoo priest, to use death magic on Katherine, whose husband she wants. By herself, Celie is powerless in operating the material and nonmaterial worlds to achieve the consequences she desires.

The battle between the two women becomes a battle between restraint (Katherine) and the lack of it (Celie). This battle calls into being the principle of Nommo (the word), which Bantu scholar Alexis Kagame identifies as one of the primary principles of African ontology[21] and, adds Molefi Asante, is "the generative and productive power of the spoken word."[22] Through word power, a human being can effect and command changes. Celie utters words with no influence. She belittles ex-slaves including Dahomey, the Voodoo priest, who refuses to do her bidding and reminds her that her tongue is a viper and her enemy. Unconscious of the effect of her words, Celie fails to realize that "[t]here is no 'harmless,' noncommittal word. Every word has consequences. Therefore, the word binds the Muntu (human being). And the Muntu is responsible for [his/her] word."[23] Moreover, Celie's single voice in a Voodoo rite renders her ineffective. Her participation in the rite without Dahomey[24] shows her disrespect for him and for ancient Voodoo ceremonies, in which, according to custom, the high priest and a female native, referred to as King and Queen, function as the media through which the snake, as supernatural being, predicts the future. In Dahomey's absence, Celie utilizes in the Voodoo ritual a snake that bites her. The bite symbolizes her improper spiritual connection with the Divinity in Dahomey's absence and her familiarity with only the external aspects of Voodoo.

Katherine applies the self-control that Celie has failed to. She wills her anger to be subdued in the face of Celie's evil. She chooses her words carefully and speaks honestly. She even administers aid to Celie for the snakebite and makes it clear that even the wicked deserve to live. Masking her anger, Katherine communicates her moral obligation to Celie as a human, and her sense of morality lifts her above the morally depraved Celie, who makes it known that she would not have done the same for Katherine. Katherine's quiet revolt points to Celie's lack of penance which leads ultimately to Celie's spiritual and physical death. A good woman who pities Celie for wanting what she cannot have, Katherine represents the value of the black pearl, the priceless necklace that Celie covets but is passed on to Katherine as Martin's wife.

In her race/gender/class struggles simulating the difficulties of a sociohistorical gestation, Katherine brings to term a new identity. She emerges as a gem in the community, one who has revolutionized the medical profession with her herbs and adherence to the African Living Belief System. Her voice becomes that of communal memory as she honors past generations and celebrates future ones in the birth of her daughter, Delpha Annalise. Her presence in Francine Craft's *The Black Pearl* offers a new perspective and image of the black female herbalist in the historical romance genre.

Beverly Jenkins's Dr. Lancaster in *Vivid*

Beverly Jenkins' *Vivid* also focuses on the black woman's call to heal, but unlike *The Black Pearl,* it revisits the history of the first generation of formally trained black women physicians in the United States. It therefore expands the literary presentation of the black female health care professional from nurse to physician in black literature. Generated by nineteenth-century medical history, the novel offers important insight into forces that shaped the character of nineteenth-century black female medical professionals. A brief look at the history lays the foundation for the heroine's significance.

Black women physicians, similar to their white female counterparts, entered a predominantly white male profession and were barred from coed matriculation in major medical schools. Their early entry into the medical profession was through the irregular medical schools (homeopathy, Eclectic) and female medical colleges. In 1864, Rebecca Lee, a Richmond, Virginia, native, became the first black woman to receive her medical degree from New England Female Medical College in Boston; and in 1867, Rebecca J. Cole, a Philadelphia native, was graduated from Woman's Medical College of Pennsylvania, considered the first regular female medical school. Prior to the twentieth century, those black women who neither matriculated at regular medical schools nor attended female medical colleges received their training at historically black Howard University Medical School, Washington, D.C.; Meharry Medical School, Nashville; Leonard Medical School (at Shaw University), Raleigh, North Carolina; New Orleans University Medical School; and Knoxville (Tenn.) Medical College. Black women's successful graduation from these schools neither guaranteed their residency at black hospitals, which preferred men, nor assured them positions at women's hospitals, which favored white women. Doctoring was considered a male profession.

In the face of general discrimination against female doctors, black women entered the medical field under the specter of racist theories espoused by one of America's leading physicians, Benjamin Rush (1754–1813), and adhered to until the end of the nineteenth century. Rush's theory of negritude, mentioned in *Vivid*, speculates that the color of black skin is a form of leprosy.[25] In a presentation to the American Philosophical Society on July 14, 1792, Rush argued, "Our fellow creatures who are known by the epithet of negroes are derived from a modification of that disease which is known by the name of Leprosy."[26] According to Rush, Negroes were carriers of a mild form of congenital leprosy, with their excessive skin pigmentation appearing as their only symptom. Thomas S. Szasz states, "With this theory Rush made the Negro a medically safe domestic while at the same time called for his social sexual segregation as a carrier of a dreaded hereditary disease."[27] Few whites doubted Rush's theory of negritude. An outstanding medical physician, father of American psychiatry, dean of the medical school at the University of Pennsylvania, signer of the Declaration of Independence, and an abolitionist, Rush laid the racial foundation that contributed to the exclusion of blacks in America's medical schools, hospitals, and clinics.

Black women doctors, then, needed not only an education but also a resilient character to scale the walls of race and gender exclusion in American medicine. Beverly Jenkins's *Vivid* illuminates just such hard times and resiliency in the depiction of Dr. Viveca Lancaster, certified in women's and children's health.

The name "Dr. Viveca Lancaster" announces the strength of the doctor's character as well as her class status. Affixed to the title Dr., the name introduces a black woman who has stepped outside the social boundaries ascribed to female members of the race. She has dared to obtain a medical degree, which places her on equal footing with white women and with white and black men. Some of her strength is borne in the confluence of ethnicities that make up her heritage. The Spanish first name "Viveca" and the European surname "Lancaster" merge the dual cultures of her ancestors, who forged an uncommon legacy for their descendants. Her great-great grandfather Esteban (of Moorish descent) and his wife Maria, a Spanish slave with Ethiopian ancestors, were among those few families who founded Los Angeles, California, a Spanish settlement. Then, too, her strength is derived from her masculine actions. She plays billiards and poker and shoots a rifle.

Affectionately called "Vivid" by relatives and friends, Dr. Lancaster exhibits a fullness of life that renders her competent in everything she does. As heroine, Dr. Lancaster is cast as the classmate of the real-life Carrie Still Wiley Anderson,[28] a black woman who was graduated from the prestigious Woman's Medical College of Philadelphia but, due to racism, was restricted to practice only in the black community. Dr. Lancaster is initially denied her internship and then receives it at Boston's New England Hospital for Women and Children after graduating from Woman's Medical College in 1875.[29] She makes a cross-country train journey from California to Michigan in 1876 to assume a medical post in a small, isolated black town called Grayson Grove in Niles, Michigan. As physician, Dr. Lancaster brings to fiction what Dr. Carrie Anderson and her classmates brought to history—an unforgettable character of self-determination.

That Dr. Lancaster travels alone testifies to her fortitude and adaptability. She knows when and when not to choose to fight. She minimizes her segregated accommodations, first on a soot-filled bench in an isolated boxcar and then in a noisy, smelly smoking car. Supplanting the authority of the racist train conductor who assigns her to segregated quarters, Dr. Lancaster achieves her ultimate desire—to reach her destination and set up her medical practice.

Dr. Lancaster transports and fertilizes her desire on the Central Pacific train (a phallic symbol), reinforcing her passage into a traditionally male profession. She wins the protection of a black gambler who functions as the male copula easing her frustrations as a woman traveling alone. She revels in male camaraderie at a poker game and appears down-to-earth despite her illustrious background.

Similar to the journeys of her real-life counterparts, Dr. Viveca Lancaster's migration represents a shift from unemployment to employment. Her safe migration via a black male copula ironically links her racist encounters on the train with gender prejudice at her final destination.[30] The gender conflict spun from the superior attitudes of those males who deem medicine to be the domain of white men locates Dr. Lancaster in a history in which American women, both black and white, found difficulty penetrating the white male medical profession.

Gender is also used in this novel to stir debate about the black woman's need for self-reliance versus her need for black male protection (especially that of a husband). This argument stems from contradictory postbellum social phenomena, especially the continued subjugation of black women as blacks and the emergence of black women in self-supporting professional careers. The controversy often pitted black men and black women against each other, since black men engaged in postbellum activism to protect black women at a time when black women felt they could fend for themselves.

Dr. Viveca Lancaster and Nate Grayson, the town's mayor and romantic hero, embody these contrasting ideas—the black woman's need for self-support and her need for male protection. Overtly manifested in the clothing the two wear, the opposing ideas bring clarity to the characters. Dr. Lancaster arrives in Grayson Grove wearing an emerald-green traveling suit with a matching hat. Her clothes suggest the appropriateness of her appearance for the job she seeks, and the color of the suit indicates her professional preparedness to assume the physician's position which Grayson's Aunt Abigail has already hired her for. The suit, together with her expensive white blouse and green hat with a feather, distinguishes her role as physician from the poorly dressed domestics and the gaudily donned fancy girls (prostitutes). Dr. Lancaster's dress presents her as a self-assured middle-class woman of good taste, embarking on a new role unfamiliar to men such as Grayson.

Nate Grayson is identified by his dirty, scuffed boots. His mean, well-worn footwear is an outer manifestation of his entrenchment in a patriarchal tradition that expects women to serve and groom men. In the absence of a wife, Grayson shows by his unkempt appearance that he needs one. His own need, in the patriarchal thinking of the day, is distorted to become the woman's need for protection. His mean attitude toward the as-yet-unidentified Dr. Lancaster traveling alone reinforces his mind-set and complements his dirty boots. At the train station, for instance, he belittles Dr. Lancaster's introduction of herself as a physician and insists that he does not want to play doctor with her. Grayson's signifying on a children's game of "playing doctor" refers to Vivid's misplacement as a young woman in an older man's profession, and it hints at Grayson's preconceived notions that women do not become doctors and that those who do are not "ladies." To Grayson's thinking, even if Vivid were a doctor, she is unescorted and, therefore, is not a lady.

Stereotyped as someone other than who she really is, Viveca takes a strong stand to correct presumptive patriarchal thinking. With the combat readiness of a male, she fights Grayson as a man. She shoots his hat off in the middle of the town before wide-eyed onlookers and forces him to rethink her identity and to honor her one-year contract. In this strong display of character, Dr. Lancaster dramatizes the black woman's intent and need to work, and she sends the salient message that she knows how to protect herself and does not need a man.

Dr. Lancaster encounters gender biases throughout the Grayson Grove community. Nate Grayson, the town's patriarch, believes only men should be physicians; Dr. Wadsworth Hayes, Viveca's near-blind white competitor, bleeds his patients and refuses to acknowledge Viveca as a physician; and other community men separate themselves from women's work in the house—all oppose Dr. Lancaster as a female physician. These men embody the nineteenth-century idea that the "home" is the woman's "private" domain, separate and distinct from the man's "public" world of wage earning, politics, fishing, and hunting. This socially constructed gender prejudice seems consistent with the vulnerability of Dr. Lancaster's women patients. For nineteenth-century black women especially, gender bias against them was linked primarily to their roles as mother and homemaker. Their woman-specific and socially delegated functions were often performed in untenable situations that produced gender-specific medical problems.

As the female physician in Grayson Grove, Vivid sensitizes the community to gender issues and upgrades living conditions of her female patients. In the first instance, she works to eradicate the problem of gender exhaustion in nineteenth-century women who spent long hours engaged in repetitive and monotonous daily tasks in the home. Her patient is nineteen-year-old Jewel Crowley, unmarried and an only daughter, who has collapsed from fatigue. Having assumed the responsibility of her dead mother, Jewel has cared for her five grown robust brothers and her equally robust father. Appalled by Jewel's physical condition, Dr. Lancaster scolds the Crowley men for leaving all the housework for Jewel to do. Assuming that Jewel has been forced into performing tasks by herself, Dr. Lancaster has misjudged the men, who make clear that Jewel has performed all the housework herself because she can do it better and quicker. In fact, it takes her one-sixth of the time that it takes her brothers to perform the same task. Dr. Lancaster, however, refuses to let her misjudgment and Jewel's efficiency absolve the men of their responsibilities.

Sensitizing the Crowleys to gender issues, Dr. Lancaster operates on two fronts. She engages men in house chores and she appeals to Jewel to allow her brothers and father to help her with the chores. The doctor's intervention strikes down the notion of the separation of the woman's private sphere from the man's public domain, and she undermines the female work ethic that some mothers pass on to their daughters, subjecting them to a second-class position in the home. Dr. Lancaster reeducates Jewel by assuring her that the promise she made to her mother to care for her brothers and father did not mean she should work herself to death.

The strength of Dr. Lancaster's character is witnessed in the physical work she offers to do for the Crowleys during Jewel's illness. Housework to her is not offensive, but neither is it gender specific. Dr. Lancaster launders the clothes, weeds the garden, and plants spring vegetables with the help she elicits from the Crowley men. The doctor's work appears all the more significant because it attacks the patriarchal assumption of the division of labor that has its origin in Christianity. Mr. Crowley, the father of the clan, is a Christian patriarch with specific notions about gender. With his home filled with dirty dishes and smelly, unwashed clothing, he's more concerned about marrying the doctor off to any one of his five sons, all of whom bear the names of biblical patriarchs—Noah, Abraham, Ezekiel, Jeremiah, and Paul—than he is with performing household duties. While Mr. Crowley signifies on Frederick Douglass—regarding him as always waiting for someone else to be first—Mr. Crowley signifies on himself and makes his chauvinism toward his "enslaved" daughter all the more repulsive. His Christian, though patriarchal, sensibilities are linked to the historically patriarchal position of the community's Bethel A.M.E Church[31] and to the Bible, which commands women to become helpmeets to men.

Dr. Lancaster manifests her strength in another medical situation—a house call to Sara James, a young sickly mother lying on a filthy sofa and cradling her infant who has been dead for two weeks. Leaving the dark, hot, dilapidated cabin that reeks of sweat and rot, Vivid confronts the surly husband in the yard and censures him for knowing his child is dead but doing nothing about it. Implying the responsibility of the husband to bury the child, Dr. Lancaster meets resistance from a husband angered by his wife's infidelity. Acknowledging that his wife had given birth before his return from a fishing trip a week earlier, Mr. James confirms that his wife delivered the baby herself in her own filth. Dr. Lancaster's confrontation with Sara James's husband illuminates the extent of the separation of the woman's world from that of the man.

The doctor learns that Mr. James's absence from the home for months left a lonely Sara James. Refusing to bury the infant or care for his three-year-old, the husband plans to move to Muskegon, which he regards as a great place for men. Giving the doctor the freedom to do whatever she wants with his wife, Mr. James leaves. Alternating between trembling and grave emotion, Dr. Lancaster digs the grave, inters the dead infant, and contacts a female relative to care for Sara and her toddler. The inhumanity of Sara's situation motivates Dr. Lancaster to perform tasks unrelated to her profession.

The sheer magnitude of Dr. Lancaster's work reveals an untiring activist. She examines the sick, normalizes the households of sick women, operates a clinic at the church, collects individual medical histories from the community folk, and lectures on measles and proper nutrition. Her payment for services is often rendered in produce and farm animals. Yet, her belief in racial and gender equality drives her to uplift women in the home. Empowering others, Dr. Lancaster manifests her social awareness of and urgent need to correct dismal situations and statistics regarding women's health in nineteenth-century America.

Dr. Lancaster is a fictional counterpart to nineteenth-century female physicians who delivered children, assisted the midwife in difficult births, and attended women who had no assistance with the birthing process. These doctors found babies with respiratory diseases, gastrointestinal diseases, and birth defects as serious as hydrocephalus.[32] They treated women patients with puerperal fever, tumors, hemorrhaging, prolapsed uteruses, and vesicovaginal fistula (anal and vaginal incontinence). Poverty, ignorance, poor genes, disease, and malnourished pregnant black women who had had no prenatal care contributed to the infant and maternal fatality rates. Statistics for black infant mortality were not kept until 1900, but the troubling figures for that year mirror the losses that had occurred earlier in the black community. In 1900, for every 1,000 live black births, 344.5 black children under the age of one year died, compared with 159.4 white infant deaths.[33] Life expectancy for the black female at birth, in 1900, was 33.5 years, compared with 48.7 for the white female.[34] Given the circumstances of the time, it seems reasonable that expectancy rates would be even lower in the mid-1870s, nearly a quarter of a century earlier, when *Vivid* is set. These startling statistics, coupled with poor living conditions and general ignorance about hygiene, made the presence of black women physicians in the nineteenth century all the more important. And a female physician with the spirit and resilience of Dr. Lancaster proved to be a necessity.

Basic to Dr. Lancaster's doctoring is the concept of new-age cleanliness. Receiving her degree after 1850, Dr. Lancaster represents the shift in medicine from bleeding to using antiseptics. Her position contrasts that of Benjamin Rush, who bled his patients as a curative. Rush believed that diseases resulted from a buildup of noxious miasmas in the body and that to rid the body of these impurities, he had to bleed his patients. Later, he taught, "There is but one disease in the world" and that the essential cause of an illness was "vascular tension."[35] To relieve the tension, Rush bled his patients until four-fifths of the blood was removed.[36] He mistakenly thought that he had broken a fever when the bled patient broke out in a profuse sweat. At the height of the 1793 yellow fever epidemic in America's port cities, Rush bled and purged his patients, many of whom died either from the seriousness of the fever or the drastic therapeutics that he employed.

Dr. Lancaster functions as a foil to Dr. Wadsworth Hayes, her white male competitor and parodic representation of Dr. Rush. In one of the most dramatic and traumatic scenes in *Vivid,* Dr. Lancaster struggles with Dr. Hayes, called in by Sara James's husband to leech and bleed Sara's three-year-old toddler. Unable to obtain the cause of the child's illness from her colleague, Dr. Lancaster is horrified by the cruelty of the bleeding. She rushes toward the child to extract the leeches from the child's face as the mouths of the parasites rip away patches of skin. Screaming her outrage, Dr. Lancaster is forcibly removed from the room and carried outside by Nate Grayson. Dr. Hayes proceeds with the bloodletting, and the child dies.

In contrast to Dr. Hayes, Dr. Lancaster adheres to the theories of Dr. Joseph Lister (1827–1912), an English surgeon who advocated cleanliness as a means to ward off pathogenic organisms. Lister believed that exposure to germs in the air caused the formation of pus, and, in 1867, he advocated the use of the antiseptic agent carbolic acid during surgery to keep the wound free of germs.[37] Similarly, Dr. Lancaster stresses cleanliness. Her medical kit includes bottles of carbolic solution, which Dr. Lister recommended for keeping wounds and instruments clean. Believing that germs in the air cause sickness, she covers her nose from the stench in the Crowleys' home and nearly retches from the odor in the James's cabin. An admirer of Dr. Lister's work, Vivid expects Lister's antiseptic methods will find favor among other physicians in the United States, despite American physicians' fierce debate over his techniques during the historical era in which *Vivid* is set. In reality, it was not until the 1890s that American physicians accepted Lister's antiseptic practices.

Dr. Lancaster's strong views and her diligence as a physician induce romance at the medical site. Her attention to her patients gains the respect of the authoritative Nate Grayson, whose concern about Viveca's two-day absence causes him to interrupt the doctor's work at the Crowley home. Grayson's unexpected visit to the Crowleys combined with his referencing Vivid first as "doctor" and then as "Viveca" announces finally his recognition of her as a physician and his interest in her as a woman. His concern about Vivid stems from her prioritizing her medical work rather than massaging his ego as other women in the town have done. But more important, Grayson, as patriarch, regards Dr. Lancaster's willful absence as a threat to his own black male dominance and to his lack of control of her, whom he has grown to admire.

Viveca insists upon her independence and self-identity. Her dogged individualism allows her to work as a female physician in a predominantly male profession and express her sexuality as a woman in the romance. This contrariety metaphorically manifests itself in her mannish attire when she performs "woman's" work. She dons an oversized red plaid shirt and denim trousers which accentuate the curvature of her hips and her pleasing leg structure. Wearing pants, she cleans her office, runs errands, and calls on patients. What the professional persona conceals is a lush womanhood leading to male-female intimacies in the novel that black women's historical romances written during or around the nineteenth century avoided because of strict standards of that time. In an intimate moment with Grayson, Vivid fully undresses and brazenly offers herself to him. This intimacy permits a fuller development of the black female protagonist's sexuality and expands the parameters for gender portrayal in African American literature. That Dr. Lancaster reserves her sexuality exclusively for Grayson enhances her relationship with him and brings an unsought-after marriage proposal. But more important, her sexuality upgrades the nineteenth-century image of the black female character from a one-dimensional "unsexed" agent to a fully rounded manager of her own life. The way in which Vivid is distinguished here has significance for our time, especially since women today believe they have the right to express their sexuality fully.

Dr. Lancaster disapproves of class superficialities that label and stifle black women's sexuality. For the doctor, "class" means dedicating oneself to one's profession for the good of the community, rather than signifying on another's private life and using bloodline, color caste, and material possessions as a barometer to measure whether or not a person is "good." Class, then, is used in this novel as an inhibitor of black progress. This point is demonstrated when the dark-skinned Dr. Lancaster objects to superficialities of class important to a group of white-looking, white-behaving colored churchwomen who put much stock in their accumulation of gaudy material assets in imitation of white capitalists, but who contribute nothing to the less fortunate members of the race. Dr. Lancaster not only demonstrates—with her mixed Spanish, African, and European heritage—that she has the best bloodline, but she also answers the rigid inquiries about her breeding via her expert tea serving, piano playing, and professional work with the ill and poverty stricken. What Dr. Lancaster proves to these light-complexioned pietists is that pseudo appearances of class are more of a hindrance to racial uplift and unity than a dark complexion, poverty, or a single woman's private sex life. Her sentiment predates the late-nineteenth-century uplift work of Josephine St. Pierre Ruffin, founder of the New Era Club and assailant of those whites, especially men, who espoused a low opinion about black women's morality.[38] Dr. Lancaster's actions suggest that natural, consensual sex between responsible men and women should not be denied for the purpose of deconstructing negative white patriarchal views of black women's sexuality.

Dr. Lancaster's "birth" as black woman medical physician in Grayson Grove heralds an expulsion of antiquated notions about race, gender, and class. She brings death to racism when the white Dr. Hayes is run out of town, she eliminates sexist thinking by appealing to a generation of younger women to avoid health risks, and she redefines class for concerned black women. Politicizing the issues of race, gender, and class, Dr. Viveca Lancaster, as medical physician, functions as a prototype character in African American literature.

Depictions of Dr. Viveca Lancaster in *Vivid* and Katherine Keyes in *The Black Pearl* clearly indicate the historical and social circumstances surrounding the lives of black nineteenth-century women healers and physicians. Both women confronted racism, sexism, and classism at an historical moment when America's medical profession was beset with internal skepticism, conflict, and impractical solutions. Caring primarily for black women and children whose illnesses were statistically ignored and medically mismanaged in the nineteenth century, Dr. Lancaster and Katherine Keyes often put their private romantic lives on hold to give inestimable medical help to others. Their characters offer an expanded look at black female health professionals in black literature, and their call to heal was another form of black women's nineteenth-century activism.

4 Post-Reconstruction Activism

The Call to Be Educated and to Educate

Beverly Jenkins's Cara Henson and Shirely Hailstock's Clara Winslow

Post-Reconstruction witnessed black women's continued struggle to educate the black masses. Following in the footsteps of pre–Civil War and Civil War black pedagogues Mary Smith Kelsey Peake[1] and E. Belle Mitchell Jackson,[2] late-nineteenth-century teachers such as Anna Julia Cooper[3] and Fanny Jackson Coppin[4] inherited a history of educational disenfranchisement of blacks that had nourished and perpetuated slavery. As one slave woman, Hannah Crasson, admitted, "The white folks did not allow us to have nothing to do with books. You better not be found trying to read. Our marster was harder down on that than anything else. You better not be catched with a book."[5] Knowing that her slave master considered book learning to be inappropriate for slaves, Crasson avoided severe punishment by not learning to read or write.

White southern attitudes about educating blacks changed little after slavery, despite postwar efforts of the Freedmen's Bureau and the American Missionary Association to educate blacks. When the Union Army withdrew from the South in 1877, ending Reconstruction, 95 percent of blacks were still illiterate, and fewer than one-third of southern black children in the 1880s received a free education.[6] Inequitable monetary expenditures in favor of whites' education were the norm, and white terrorism endangered the lives of black and white teachers who taught blacks in the South. Despite these hardships for young black teachers, black educator Fanny Jackson Coppin encouraged her women students graduating from the Institute of Colored Youth in Baltimore in 1879 to take teaching jobs. But she warned them that school districts needing them most would pay them least.[7]

Some black teachers fled the South to embrace new frontiers in the West, especially Kansas and Montana. Joining the Exodusters movement in the 1880s, which set out to build independent black communities in the western states, many young teachers embodied the notion that education is the great equalizer. They braved inhospitable environments, founded and operated schools, planned curricula, taught overcrowded classes, and received little pay. Black women educators became a visible and formidable force; they laid the foundation for black education in outposts where no schools existed for blacks.

The racial imperative that called black women to educate themselves and to educate others met with gender obstacles. The last third of the nineteenth century proved an era of resistance to the education of American women, generally based on their physiology. In 1874, Dr. Edward H. Clarke, medical physician and fellow of the American Academy of Arts and Sciences, argued that a menstruating female who engaged in brain work made herself susceptible to a "host of ills," including "periodic hemorrhage, . . . amenorrhoea, monorrhagia, dysmenorrhoea, hysteria, anemia [and] chorea."[8] This male-centered notion of separating the woman's head (intellect) from her body (reproductive organs) was common in nineteenth-century literature and became a primary issue that nineteenth-century black and white women educators argued vehemently against.

As early as 1884, Josephine J. Turpin, a black Virginia essayist in defense of women's education, wrote, "The very fact that woman has a mind capable of infinite expansion is in itself an argument that she should receive the highest possible development."[9] Turpin and other black women had as much reason to speak out against sexism in their own racial group as they did in voicing objection to the gender bias in the larger community. They lagged behind black men in receiving a collegiate education. By 1900, black women composed only 14 percent of the graduates from black colleges. Black women with baccalaureate degrees numbered 252 compared with 2,272 black men.[10] The educational discrepancy stemmed from years of sexism in an already racially segregated educational system and illustrated the imperative for women to obtain a higher education in order to uplift themselves and their charges. Convincingly, Turpin argued for women's education to bring about their mental and physical empowerment when their male counterparts believed that educating females would lead to their physical deterioration.

Racism and sexism were not the only barriers that prospective black teachers struggled to overcome. They also confronted class discrimination. Class discrimination among blacks was linked to education and to the lighter-hued members of the race. Prejudice against the darker-hued black was fostered during slavery when some light-complexioned slaves were privileged with an education denied their darker-hued counterparts. The situation that Sylvia Cannon, a Florence, South Carolina, slave, describes in the introduction (p. 9) was typical for much of the white South, which had punishing restrictions against educating slaves. When light-complexioned slaves were educated, it would not have been unusual for them to regard their learning as a means for them to elevate themselves above the illiterate darker hued.

By the time of post-Reconstruction, black women of all shades had entered the teaching profession, and the black teaching post carried a class agenda. Financial independence and morality, often perceived as inseparable by-products of good social standing, became the touchstones of class. A paying job signifying financial success hoisted the black woman teacher to a superior place within the colored social stratum and garnered for her respect from the economically disadvantaged. Her moral carriage separated her from the illiterate masses traditionally perceived to have low morals. In a speech signed "Calx" and addressed to the members-elect of the General Assembly of Virginia in 1859, for instance, blacks were considered a demoralized lot, not worthy of freedom: "There can be no question of the general truth, that the free negroes, as a class, are ignorant, lazy, and improvident. . . . Very many are drunkards, and more are partly supported by petty thefts and other violations of law, or of morality. . . . The young females are rarely chaste, and in many cases the mulattoes are habitual prostitutes."[11] Calx's speech clearly shows the perceived relationship between poverty and immorality. The history of racial stereotyping evident in Calx's speech led black school officials and concerned community residents to endorse and vigorously enforce morality strictures for their young female teachers as a way to disprove whites' notions of blacks' immorality.

Young black female teachers were expected to be paragons of virtue as moral decorum became a primary requisite for teaching. The darker-hued teacher came under as much scrutiny as her lighter-complexioned counterpart, since her color most represented the stigma attached to the race's alleged debasement. Unmarried black female teachers were forced to sign contracts that forbade kissing in public, required chaperones to community functions, and opposed fornication and pregnancy. Their restrictions were similar to those of their white counterparts, but for a different reason. Chastity was required for young black women teachers to avert racist perceptions of them as whores, yet class expectations contrasted sharply with the reality of youth, who naturally exuded a sexual presence. Even as strictures germane to class often invalidated the sexuality of black women teachers, these instructors nevertheless pursued a mission to uplift the race. Ironically, the argument of discontinuity between mind and body that some male proponents used to keep black women out of the teaching profession later became justification for continuance of their jobs.

Black women teachers have had a long history in African American women's literature, from Frances Harper's Minnie LeCroix in *Minnie's Sacrifice* (1869), Annette Miller in *Trial and Triumph* (1888–89), and the title character in *Iola Leroy* (1892) to Mem in Alice Walker's *The Third Life of Grange Copeland* (1970) and Zora Banks in Terry McMillan's *Disappearing Acts* (1989). With 130 years separating McMillan's fiction from Harper's first novel, the black woman teacher as fictional character has been presented as an entity separate from and foreign to the stresses of her profession. While it is true that white terrorists torched Iola Leroy's schoolhouse and put her out of a job, black teachers in African American literature have generally been portrayed as tokens signifying race progress rather than as workers experiencing stress in the workplace. Issues related to inadequate funding of black education, unapproved curriculum changes, bias against coeducation of the sexes, stereotyping of the female teacher, unfair contract policies, and sexuality and class concerns have been issues excluded from the teaching profession in black women's fiction prior to the publication of recent historical romances.

So, too, were the personal or private lives of black women teachers excluded from black fiction until the advent of the women's liberation movement in the late 1960s. This movement had a significant impact on American women's literature, which began to illuminate some women's issues for the first time. In African American literature, two novels come to mind wherein black women teachers' private lives are exposed—Walker's *The Third Life of Grange Copeland,* in which Mem's husband beats and brutally murders her because she improves her life as a teacher, and McMillan's *Disappearing Acts,* in which Zora's live-in boyfriend interferes with her effectiveness as a music teacher. While these novels expose black male abuse of black women within the home, they do not address an equally important issue—the community's condemnatory stance against what it perceived as the "bad" teacher; that is, one who satisfied her intellectual and physical needs. The failure of African American literature in ignoring the private and personal needs of black women as teachers was its failure to record the full struggle of nineteenth-century black women educators.

Beverly Jenkins's *Night Song* (1994) and Shirley Hailstock's *Clara's Promise* (1995) illuminate black women's stress and struggles in their teaching professions and the community's involvement in young black teachers' personal lives. These narratives reveal black women teachers' vigorous post-Reconstruction fight for their rights to be educated and to educate and to conduct their private lives without outside interference. As character studies, the narratives show how black heroines Cara Lee Henson in *Night Song* and Clara Winslow in *Clara's Promise* challenge nineteenth-century stereotypes of black women teachers as paragons of virtue at the same time that they contend with other education-related issues. Varying from the perceived "good" image expected of young teachers, Cara and Clara are portrayed as daring, sometimes foolhardy young women. In their efforts to develop their minds and bodies, they meet more challenges than their nineteenth-century literary counterparts.

The presence of Cara Lee Henson and Clara Winslow in these historical romances expands the image of black teachers as activists in African American literature in four specific ways. First, these heroines regard race, gender, and class as repressive social controls which must be overcome in order for the black woman teachers to obtain a genuine public identity. Second, the heroine-teacher migrates great distances from the South to the West as a form of protest, a journey whose length matches the depth of the heroine's desire to teach and one that broadens the geographical borders for nineteenth-century black women activist educators, who generally traveled from the South to the North in African American women's fiction. Cara Lee Henson in *Night Song* migrates from Georgia to Henry Adams Township, Kansas; Clara Winslow in *Clara's Promise* migrates from Virginia to Waymon Valley, Montana. Third, these heroines oppose more vigorously than their nineteenth-century literary counterparts the then-current male-centered notions that denied females an education and a public role in the educational arena. Cara Lee Henson refuses to separate her intellectual self from her reproductive self, and Clara Winslow rejects marital sex to educate herself and others. Fourth, despite class and community strictures to disprove whites' notions of black women's immorality, the heroines affirm their sexuality, whereas their literary counterparts in African American women's nineteenth-century fiction did not. As activists, both Cara Lee Henson and Clara Winslow illustrate black women's bold fight to overcome odds in the teaching profession while they define themselves as women.

The Call to Teach in Kansas: Beverly Jenkins's Cara Lee Henson

Twenty-four-year-old Cara Lee Henson, a feisty and motivated teacher, comes alive in a plot whose story line dramatizes blacks' exodus to and settlement in Kansas to escape white mob violence following the Union soldiers' withdrawal from the South in 1877. A Georgia native, she settles in Henry Adams Township, Kansas, a fictitious site named after a former slave and Union soldier[12] and the sister township to the real-life Nicodemus,[13] the first black Kansas community, established in 1877 on the south fork of the Solomon

River. Cara's affinity to the other 'dusters[14] in this town resides in her childhood background of racial victimization, made evident by the omniscient narrator. At nine years old, she witnessed Union soldiers lynching her grandfather, a free black landowner and her only guardian, because they thought he had lied about not having a master. She lived in an orphanage and hid in trees to escape the midnight raids of the Ku Klux Klan. Her inability to stay the execution of her grandfather or prevent the soldiers from burning down his property is akin to the real-life helplessness of one southern black woman who lamented during post-Reconstruction, "O, Lord, God of Hosts, help us to get out of this country and get somewhere where we can live," when sixty white terrorists fatally burned her husband because he did not relinquish his constable position.[15]

Whether the race hatred Cara witnessed stemmed from the Union soldiers' misconceptions of blacks or from the vanquished southerners' strategy to regain and maintain white privilege, color difference provoked the violence in both instances. Cara's response to white oppression has been defiance. Her rebellious character was shaped as a child under the careful tutelage of Rosetta Sterling, her surrogate mother, race leader, and orphanage proprietor, and of Harriet Bat, Sterling's assistant. Together, Sterling and Bat embody a tough masculine resistance necessary to prepare Cara for her adult years. By seventeen years of age, Cara had been arrested for rallying, had championed the vote for black men, and had chastised officials at the local Freedmen's Bureau for the horrible conditions of the colored schools they managed. Throwing her energy into positive activities against racism, Cara has always aimed to change situations for the better. She considers herself to be brash, educated, and argumentative. These traits are the hallmarks of protest that caused her to lose her first teaching job in Blessed, Ohio, where she violated the rules and educated females. Since Cara has inherited her strong masculine-like dissent from her surrogate mother and her grandfather, it can be said that a male-fired copula provides Cara the incentive for her journeys, including that to Henry Adams Township.

Cara Henson becomes a fictional construct identified with the approximately 40,000 Exodusters who historian Robert G. Athearn estimates settled in Kansas in the 1870s.[16] Her migration manifests her conscious refusal to accept repressive control and her longing for identification as a black woman. Her movement to the West is made in the attempt to create a new life for herself, and the journey occurs with a predominantly black male political front. Expecting to expand her personal boundaries and minimize conflict, Cara soon discovers that her hopes contrast with reality in Henry Adams Township. A vibrant, outgoing person, Cara finds herself in an impoverished, religion-dominated, all-black township that exerts even more control over her as a teacher than she had formerly endured. This narrow setting manifests all the more her rebellious desire for growth even as she experiences the gestational pangs of a teaching career.

Cara deplores the economic hardship that limits her professional instruction and causes her tension. Assessing the problem is her first step to dealing with her tension. She teaches thirty-five black and Native American students in an old church converted into a cramped and patched one-room schoolhouse. Her library of unpacked books is meager and dangerous, and her materials limited. Her plight as teacher is a fictional reenactment of historical fact of what occurred during blacks' settlement in the West. Race difference kept the 'dusters of 1879 poor and their institutions undeveloped. Their per capita assets at the end of 1879 were approximately $2.25 per person,[17] and these assets could do little to provide adequate schools. To add insult to poverty, white farmers in Kansas prevented their children from race mixing in the public schools for fear of blacks' inferiority and immorality.[18]

Taking direct action to bring change is Cara's next step. She transforms her desire for a successful instructional career into positive action. She writes to Aid Societies back East for donations. Her bold attempt to collect money for black education is a strike against state and federal neglect of black education after Reconstruction. Her efforts win her exceptional praise but fail to bring her the needed money. The failure is not in Cara, but in the event. Cara's presence in this narrative corroborates the efforts of nineteenth-century philanthropists John F. Slater[19] and Anna T. Jeanes,[20] who saw as their mission the mitigation of the appalling inequities in black education due to blatant racism.

Since Cara does not obtain money for her school, she cannot effect change in the local saloon, called the Liberian Lady. A trope on the West African country settled by freed slaves, the local saloon provokes Cara's wrath as a place where her twelve-year-old male students are allowed to order drinks and consort with the whores. Threatening public censure of the saloon owner, Cara corrects the ironic nineteenth-century notion that Liberia was an acceptable haven for the weary black male. A place of unrest, malnourishment, and debauchery, the Liberian Lady exists as a dumping ground for the dispossessed and a misplaced African culture.

Racism evident in separate and unequal education for blacks intersects gender and presents for Cara another tense situation in her struggle for identification. Her foil is Chase Jefferson, the slaveborn Mississippian and sergeant of the Tenth Calvary, who joined the army to obtain the legal right to carry a gun and to protect himself. Racism predisposes Chase to assert his manhood over Cara despite, or perhaps because of, his diminution as a black man in the eyes of whites. White generals and politicians have told Chase that blacks are genetically incompetent to become commissioned officers. Wearing the blue military uniform that symbolizes white aggression and exaggerating his black male prowess, Chase becomes the agent through which Cara experiences gender oppression. Combined with his name, "Chase," which suggests a hunt and capture, the military uniform gives Chase leverage for gender diversion that leads to public kissing and serious consequences for Cara.

Cara's gender dilemma gives rise to the complexity of her character. Living during a time when the black woman's sexuality is challenged by white racists and by black men, Cara has agreed to accept a teacher's contract with a morality and conduct clause that restricts her social contacts for the purpose of ennobling black womanhood. Yet she ignores the contract. The contract puts her in what Marilyn Frye calls a double bind and exposes her to penalty whether she follows it or not.[21] If Cara ignores the contract, her encounters with Chase could be misinterpreted; she could be deemed a loose woman and lose her job. If she honors the contract, Chase will tag her with the asexual label "schoolmarm," and she will be acquiescing to a gender-oppressive situation. Cara's plight typifies nineteenth-century bias that demanded the denial of a young black woman's sexuality as a prerequisite for racial uplift and virtuous black womanhood while it tolerated the dalliance and sexual indiscretions of young black men.

Cara fails to debate the issue of virtue and sin in this religious township populated with nominal and active African Methodist Episcopalians. Instead, she renegotiates the power position in her relationship with Chase. She asserts her sexuality in an act that presages her maturation as a woman. She seems to suggest that desire is personal and should not be controlled by societal norms. Since she cannot control affection, she mocks any attempt to control it. Her decision moves the gender issue beyond its traditional bounds for nineteenth-century black women teachers in African American women's novels and produces the climactic moment. The passion leads to Cara's pregnancy, the ultimate stigma and racial debasement. Her self-defining actions exempt her from becoming a victim of sexual abuse, but indict her instead for wantonness.

Cara is not a tragic character, however. She willfully delays the sexual act until she falls in love with Chase, and her decision to copulate erases from her mind a casual affair. Her later decision to move even farther west and rear the child alone suggests a woman with remarkable resolve. Her strength in a town with weak, manipulative men indicates the unimportance she attributes to the male figure in actualizing her growth. Seeming to have the issue of gender resolved, she is forced to face yet another emergence.

Gender issues merge with class issues when Cara's pregnancy leads to a formal dismissal. Class as a societal norm implicates the concept of "ladyhood," which for nineteenth-century black women meant possessing moral propriety, whereas for white women it meant having a beautifully decorated body and a respectable unemployed existence.[22] In the black community, both unemployed and employed black women who carried themselves in a respectable manner were considered "ladies." Cara, an employed, well-educated, beautiful, dark-skinned woman is a "lady" so long as she uplifts the race as a teacher and behaves in a respectable manner. When she crosses the line into what her community considers moral turpitude, she raises eyebrows about her behavior and causes a scandal.

Cara's pregnancy invokes hissing. Community members who expect Cara as a teacher to uphold the ideal standards of ladyhood call for her dismissal from her teaching duties and her loss of income. Churchwomen disapprove of her self-reliant attitude and refusal to tell Chase about her pregnancy. Ostracized as a fallen woman, Cara is determined to make her own way as an independent person. Actualizing her rebirth is a difficult struggle. The easing of her race/gender/class pain occurs through startling coincidences that do not interfere with Cara's well-being. Concurrent events establish both partners' responsibility for the consequences of premarital sex and resulting race/gender/class stigma. Chase, who has said he will never marry, marries Cara because he loves her and does not want his child to be considered illegitimate. He respects his lineage. The marriage relieves Cara of the double-standard gender myth and restores her teaching position and class status.

Despite Cara's resurrection, the reader is left with the message that black female teachers had an awesome struggle for wholeness during post-Reconstruction. Their fight for racial equality led to an intraracial struggle against gender and class bias that inconvenienced them as women on personal and public levels. What Beverly Jenkins seems to suggest in Cara Henson's portrayal is that black women's struggles for race, gender, and class advancement could have been more readily and successfully fought if black women had not been derailed by a biased community too bent on corralling them and leaving the male unbridled.

Shirley Hailstock's *Clara's Promise:* The Black Woman's Call to Be Educated and to Educate

Shirley Hailstock's Clara Winslow presents another view of post-Reconstruction black female teachers. It shows Clara Winslow's attempt to liberate herself from a patriarchal relationship that her dying father contracted for her in order to protect her from racism. Unlike Jenkins's Cara Lee Henson or Frances Harper's Iola Leroy, who secure teaching posts as single women, the married Clara Winslow assumes a teaching position only after she passes herself off as an unmarried female. Her disguise is manufactured to voice her objection to historical biases that have necessitated her loveless marriage and to the institution of marriage that denies her a right to expand her intellectual capacities. Clara Winslow shatters the neatly packaged description of black female teachers as paragons of virtue in African American literature, and she challenges contradictions inherent in the then-current arguments regarding black female education.

Anna Julia Cooper argues in her essay "The Higher Education of Women" that "both [the woman and the man] are needed to be worked into the training of children." Cooper goes on to say that "intellectual development, with the self-reliance and the capacity for earning a livelihood which it gives, renders woman less dependent on the marriage relationship for physical support. . . . Neither is she compelled to look to sexual love as the one sensation capable of giving tone and relish, movement and vim to the life she needs."[23] On the one hand, Cooper calls for the education of women for their self-reliance in marriage and for their help in educating their children; on the other hand, her argument conflicts with the reality of teaching posts in most places being closed to married women. Clara proves the flaw in Cooper's gender argument and the difficulty married women encountered as they heeded the call to be educated and to educate.

Clara's urgent need for an education stems from her desire to be less dependent on and free from the marriage relationship. Wife to Wade Pierce and stepmother to his four children (two left by his deceased wife and two by the death of his sister), Clara becomes overburdened by what her rural Virginia husband demands. She abhors the drudgery of housework and the boredom of motherhood. She regards education as a liberating force. Her insistence on naming herself "teacher" results in a conflict between actualizing self and becoming what her husband wants her to be. A partial solution to the conflict manifests Clara's determination. She walks ten miles to and ten miles from Teachers College in Washington, D.C., when her husband refuses to spare her a farm animal for passage.

Clara's obstinacy results from a racially induced gender oppression. Racism is used as an instigator of gender tension between the black woman and the black man—first between Clara and her father, who wedded her to Wade, and then between Clara and Wade. Racism breeds a sense of inadequacy in the black male, who controls the female as a means to infer value to himself. Clara refuses to become a scapegoat in the psychological race war between whites and her farmer husband. Refusing subordination to her poor, patriarchal spouse, she upsets the control he assumes over her to gain leverage for himself in the racially divided community.

Obviously, the role Clara desires for herself and the functions Wade has forced on her involve two different worlds. Clara's world demands self-definition, and the reality of her situation necessitates her having her own space to define herself. Having lived as a female in her father's house and then in Wade's, she desires her own space. To obtain that space, she severs her relationship with Wade and pursues her own life. Actualizing what she wants demands her unconventional actions. She reneges on her marriage vows and leaves Wade. Clara takes a job as a teacher in Waymon Valley, Montana, in 1899, expecting to improve herself as a poor, black woman. Wade, as male copula, induces her flight.

Clara's migration represents not only a geographical transference, but a personal transfiguration as well. She mutates to a single woman, shedding the marital trappings of husband, children, and housework without engaging in the legal ramifications necessary for her change. Violating the principle of family togetherness, an important aspect of African American culture, she appears to be an unworthy candidate for a teaching post; however, venting her frustration proves necessary for self-sufficiency and a more productive participation in the African American community. Creating a realm in which she can vent her frustration is an important lever of her resistance.

Resistance through flight to Montana, where she pursues a secret life, offers Clara a means to self-definition, upward class mobility, and engagement in racial and gender uplift. She passes herself off as an unmarried woman in a race-prejudiced area where her students are not expected to succeed because Native Americans and Negroes are not encouraged to attend college. Clara expands classroom instruction, introduces piano lessons and the blues into the limited curriculum consisting of times tables and spelling, and encourages a Native American girl to attend school. Outside the classroom, she removes the sexist barrier in sports by allowing her female students to play baseball with the boys. Challenging the school's race and gender discrimination policies, Clara reveals a moral imperative to offer an equal education and an African American cultural foundation to both sexes and all ethnic groups. She can be considered a good teacher because she develops good self-images in her students at an institution historically guilty of race and gender objectification.

Similar to Jenkins's Cara Henson, but unlike other black women teachers in African American literature, Clara experiences gestational pains in her teaching profession that interweave gender and class. The challenge is rooted in the community's expectation of her to be of "good" character and to demonstrate her "goodness" as a specific requirement of class expected of black women teachers in the new Montana territory. After all, Clara represents an era that required female teachers to be unmarried, pious, and chaste. Passing herself off as an unmarried teacher, she must not be seen kissing in public, and she must not have a man searching for her. The strictures deliberately address the possibility of sexual attraction in a male-female relationship, and they hint at the bad name that can be attached to the unmarried teacher who is not "good." These strictures also complicate the interconnection between romance and Clara's career, and they define her character as a woman.

At the center of this complication stands Luke Evans, the town's widower and builder with whom she falls in love. A patriarchal figure, Luke has standing in the town, and his wife's death has shaped his inconsistent disposition toward women, including Clara. His mind made up that he does not need another wife, Luke nevertheless expresses an interest in Clara, whom he goads into committing an infraction when he kisses her in public. This violation of the school's policy comes even as Luke knows that Clara's young age and "single" status were originally regarded by members of the school committee as factors to keep her from getting the job.

Luke's actions cause others to define Clara's character. Ironically, another woman considers Clara a harlot and starts rumors in the town. This debasement demeans her class status and suggests that women tend to berate other women in a patriarchal society for the purpose of transferring value to themselves. That Clara fails to confront her attacker is not a sign of weakness. She chooses to empower herself in the relationship with Luke on a night when she and Luke are caught in a rainstorm. Stripping away Luke's initial view of her as just another sexual object, Clara projects her own perception of herself as a woman who wants to experience and enjoy sex without pejorative labeling. Empowering herself in the relationship, she initiates the sexual act because she believes that Luke has cared enough to search for her in a driving storm. She orders Luke to make love to her. Her command reverses expectations in a male-female relationship and signals her refusal to engage in submissive sex. A self-defining character, she ignores the community's gender and class requirement for the "perfect" black female public figure in order to reveal her human, libidinal side. She never considers herself a whore because she never consummated her marriage to Wade.

Having spent the night with Luke, Clara gives rise to further rumors debasing her character. Thinking that Clara has behaved improperly with Luke, the community offers her two options, neither of which is beneficial to her: She can either give up her job or have Luke declare for her so that they can marry in the spring. Losing her job would send her back to Wade, and accepting and acting on Luke's declaration, if he offered one, would make her a bigamist. In either situation, Clara as a black woman teacher who has achieved economic independence and class status through her job will be severely compromised. The town's patriarchal censure encloses Clara in marriage and also relegates her definition as a woman to the province of her husband.

Clara arms herself with a decision to strengthen herself against her opponents. She decides that her job is secondary to her feelings about Luke. She refuses to give Luke up because of petty gossip. Clara takes a stand for what she believes in and refuses to stand for anything less. Her position may go against the community's moral codes, but it strengthens her as a woman. What completes her sense of feminine wholeness are a well-nourished mind and body.

The author's response to Clara's actions are empathetic. Hailstock sets up a final problem for Clara and then resolves it in Clara's favor. Clara becomes trapped between Wade's sudden appearance in the Valley and Luke's equally sudden decision to declare for her. She agrees to a marriage annulment and plans to marry Luke, but the author prefers to cancel the stigma of a dissolved first marriage. Deus ex machina intervenes, as is common in nineteenth-century settings, and makes Clara a widow. Wade's sudden death, however, does not absolve Clara from ethical responsibility. Death redeems Clara's character. At twenty-one years of age, she voluntarily assumes responsibility for the care of Wade's four children as a means to atone for her sins. Taking on this responsibility, she not only gets back her teaching post, but she also carries on the African tradition of sharing, a tradition which Wade has participated in and which emphasizes group collaboration rather than an acquisition of material goods. Just as Wade cared for his sons and the daughters of his dead sister, Clara cares for his children. To Clara's thinking, the children could go further in their education than their ancestors. As educator, Clara concerns herself with insulating each succeeding generation from the disappointment of the larger world.

Clara is a more self-fulfilled woman at the end of the novel than at the beginning. She has self-respect, a teaching position, and a husband whom she loves. Her rebelliousness, tenacity, and courage indicate the traits necessary for her to define herself as a woman in a world that questions the woman's right to an education and self-definition. Essentially, she delineates the complexity of the young black schoolteacher who chooses not to separate her body from her head. Eschewing the behavior expected of nineteenth-century female educators and representing values antithetical to notions of good breeding and patriarchy, Clara is a different version of the teacher in African American literature.

The image of Clara as teacher is an expansion of that of Frances Harper's Iola Leroy. A demure professional, sensitive to the ignorance of her charges, Iola Leroy as teacher sees the need to expand her curriculum by only laying "the foundation of good character"; Clara, in contrast, is more concerned about equal education for males and females and the teacher's self-identity. Moreover, Iola fails to entertain the question of her position as a single woman in a predominantly male profession and her need to balance the desires of the flesh with the desires of the mind. Clara sees these conflicting needs and fights to reconcile them. The difference between Iola Leroy and Clara Winslow lies in the authors' objectives. Harper intended Iola Leroy as a representative of what is best in the black race in order to support her claim for blacks' racial equality. Hailstock employs Clara Winslow as a political lightning rod to strike at race, gender, and class biases. In her depiction of Clara,

Hailstock argues that the woman's body in the teaching post subverts patriarchal notions of race, gender, and class rather than corrupts the profession. For this reason, Clara is an important character.

To recapitulate, Beverly Jenkins's Cara Henson and Shirley Hailstock's Clara Winslow bring to the historical romance genre and to African American literature a new and lengthy portrait of African American teachers vigorously engaged in their professions. No longer tentative status symbols identifying the race's progress, they are strong black women who define self. Their identities manifest themselves in the individual combativeness they assume to upgrade their teaching posts and to oppose the limiting, stereotypic view of virtuous black women teachers. More lifelike than mannequin, these heroines bring to the African American literary canon a broader, more realistic perspective of what nineteenth-century black women encountered as women in their teaching careers.

5 Early-Twentieth-Century Activism

Saving Land in Texas

Anita Richmond Bunkley's Leela Brannon Wilder in *Black Gold*

Studies of African American land tenancy by gender are difficult to come by. Even the Land Loss Fund, whose aim is to preserve African American landownership, tabulates its findings with no distinction between black male and female landownership.[1] Black women's invisibility in land tenancy studies is a carryover of a history of racial and patriarchal presumption that has traditionally granted land to the male household head. Historical protocol and cultural imperative have failed to acknowledge black women's ownership of land in this country for more than three hundred years.

In the years prior to the 1920s, African American women controlled a sizeable portion of farmland in the South. They obtained their land through hard work and diligent savings, as mistresses of wealthy white men, and as widows. In 1850, for instance, black women on average had accumulated more land in the South than black men. Figures for 1850 post black women's average realty assets at $1,619 compared with $1,144 for black men.[2] In Texas, for 1850, black women held one-third of the land assets.[3] By the 1920s, when approximately one out of every seven farmers in the United States was black, black women still held a sizeable portion of this farmland. However, as blacks and as women, black women belonged to two groups that culture and history disfavored as landowners in the 1920s. Their race and gender only broadened the gap between their attainment of property and society's expectation of their inequality in landownership.

Race difference has defined landownership in this country before, during, and after slavery. White men have acquired and managed their land; blacks have tilled the soil of whites. The hierarchy of power that distinguishes the landowner from the land laborer has been the key factor in preventing blacks from acquiring land and, if acquired, from keeping it. Shrewd business dealings, theft, conquests, and violence have allowed whites to seize land, even when it belongs to others of a different race. The racial presumption is that the less powerful should not have and do not deserve their own land.

With landownership comes class distinction. In a racially defined environment, landownership means dominance, prosperity, respectability, and economic security. Submission, failure, poverty, and dependence are the lot of those not fortunate enough to possess land. Such are the class lines drawn between whites and blacks, or those who have and those who do not. These negative connotations together with unreasonable low wages paid to blacks were more than enough to keep them grounded in a lower class.

Implication of race and class had negative repercussions on gender, especially when members of the dominant race and sex obtain power for themselves by seizing land deeded to those of the minority race and gender. As landowners, black women who owned land held wealth often looked upon as prosperity intended for white men and thus found their position as women landowners to be as tenuous as that of their black male counterparts. Race imperiled black women landowners who were heads of families. Social ideologies that violated the black woman's rights to economic autonomy through land tenancy impoverished her and her dependent children. Unable to provide for herself and those dependent on her, she fell into a lower-class cauldron that labeled the racial minority dependent, lazy, and poor.

In a society politically controlled by concepts of race, class, and gender, black women's maintaining rights to their land is necessary for black womanist identity and survival. Survival characteristics of black women associated with landownership include strength, hard work, perseverance—all traits of black womanism. The result of fortitude is self-sufficiency equated to economic autonomy or power. The power to choose, produce, and distribute crops determines crop-producing revenues, savings, family welfare, and livability of black women landowners and their dependents.

Anita Richmond Bunkley's *Black Gold* (1995) examines the issue of black female landownership and the applications of race, gender, and class. The novel comes 166 years after David Walker's *Appeal* (1829), in which landownership first appeared as a topic in African American literature. Since Walker's *Appeal*, which documented the difficulty race presented for black men in holding onto their property, blacks have been portrayed in African American fiction as dirt farmers (Trueblood in Ralph Ellison's *Invisible Man* and Silas in Richard Wright's "Long Black Song") and as sharecroppers (Jeff and Jennie Patton in Bontemps's "A Summer Tragedy" and Vyry Ware in Margaret Walker's *Jubilee*). Much of the fiction has focused on the black male and his determined will to survive on the land in a racist environment; little attention has been given to black women and their hard fight to save their land, especially in the absence of their husbands due to illness or death. Recording a black woman's struggle to save her own land, Anita Richmond Bunkley's *Black Gold* brings a new image to African American fiction.

Holding considerable significance in black women's fiction, *Black Gold* presents a strong black woman owning her own land. This image expands earlier depictions of black women in land-related conflicts, especially Janie Killens and her refusal to till the soil in Zora Neale Hurston's *Their Eyes Were Watching God* (1937), Vyry Ware and her struggle as a tenant farmer in Walker's *Jubilee* (1966), and Mariah Upshur in her plight to feed her family as a Maryland field hand in Sarah E. Wright's *This Child's Gonna Live* (1969). *Black Gold* debuts Leela Brannon Wilder, property owner and protagonist, who works the 340-acre farm called Rioluces during her husband's lengthy illness and then inherits it when he dies. The novel reveals Leela Wilder's encounters with race, gender, and class as landowner. These encounters and her reactions to them expand the portrait of blacks tilling the soil in African American literature.

Bunkley encases Leela's story of landownership in the historical oil boom that occurred in Mexia,[4] Texas, and the frenzy that surrounded it in the 1920s. According to the *Waco Times-Herald*, oil discovery in Mexia in 1921 brought in as much as 1,000 barrels of liquid black gold an hour.[5] In this small cotton town, the population of 3,482 increased to 55,000 in a few days as people crowded in to try their luck at the new bonanza.[6] Oil production peaked in 1922 with a total of 35,120,405 barrels for the year. As news of gushers spread, violence, thefts, and killings reached a feverish pitch.[7] In this climate, Bunkley writes about one black woman's call to keep her land despite the actions of black and white opportunists to seize it.

Leela resides on the outskirts of a developing but racially segregated town in which race and gender differences have inscribed the historical inequity of privileging land to white males. In Mexia, as in other southern towns, land owned by the white male traditionally has been passed on to his black counterpart when it has been socially, economically, and legally feasible to do so. Conversely, the white male has appropriated this same land from blacks when it has been advantageous to do so. Such is Leela's case, because her husband, Thomas Jacob Wilder (better known as T. J.), inherited his land from a neighboring white man who felt his natural son was undeserving of it; white oil speculators later seize his land. In the land game of give-and-take, black widows such as Leela Wilder have traditionally been unprotected figures because race and gender inequities have conceded legal power to the white male. Whites' demand for payment on a debt, whether real or imaginary, can financially disable vulnerable women. T. J. Wilder's debt on his farm is the source of tension in the land battle.

Leela's fight against racism and patriarchal privilege follows her migration to and residency in Mexia after the death of her father and her maternal, African grandmother who reared her. Her father, Ed Brannon, is the initiating male copula that links her to Aunt Effie, her father's sister, who resides and cares for her on the west side of town reserved for Negroes. This geographical separation of the races forced Leela as a teenager to stand her ground on issues with whites when blacks feared white reprisal. Throughout her stay with her Aunt Effie, Leela has shown no fear of whites; instead, her assertiveness makes others nervous. Her cousin Josephine, Aunt Effie's daughter, believes that Leela's brashness causes too much trouble and wishes that she would go back to wherever she came from.

Where Leela came from, she cannot go back to. Her migration to Mexia to live in her Aunt Effie's home constitutes a forward step in Leela's life. She has a roof over her head, and she is cared for as one of her aunt's children. Her arrival at Effie Alexander's home physically separates her from her African-born Grandma Ekiti, whose transient lower-class existence sharply contrasts the comfortable lower-middle-class life that Leela enjoys at the Alexanders' home. Emotionally, though, Leela is still attached to her Grandma, who has helped her to survive with little money and has taught her how to tell the truth. Essential to Leela's character is a moral base that demands she speak the truth. In a town that maintains a controlled segregation through hypocrisy, Leela discovers that truth has a price. At nineteen years old, she jeopardizes her Aunt Effie's home when she sides with her cousin Parker, Josephine's brother, instead of the vindictive white sheriff in a racial scuffle. Determined to prevent her Aunt Effie from mortgaging her home, Leela single-handedly raises $300 needed for Parker's bail. Home to Leela means comfort, security, and respectability. She values property to the extent that once she has moved into her new home, she will not allow anyone to put her out.

Leela's new home comes with her marriage to T. J., a fictional representative of the black agrarian community that Booker T. Washington urged to self-sufficiency in the latter years of the nineteenth century. Her efforts to save her land and home during her husband's illness and eventual death from consumption after eight years of marriage reinforce her value of property. Leela has a lot to fight for—her land, the prestige that goes with it, and the security of her small son.

An upper-middle-class woman whose wealth is determined by the large spread her husband owns, Leela lives with her son, before and after her husband's death, more comfortably than most blacks in Mexia. Her standard of living far exceeds that of her mother-in-law, Hattie Logan Wilder, an aging alcoholic domestic who lives in a crude lean-to and feels that she should have the right to live in her son's home and inherit his property. Ironically, the two women are each other's foil. Through a twist of circumstances tying Hattie to Leela's dead father, Hattie has stolen and cashed savings bonds that Leela's father had intended for his daughter's legacy. Leela, in turn, has usurped Hattie's place as head woman in T. J.'s home. Together, the two women represent two sides of the economic coin, both striving for identity in a capitalistic society that essentially ignores them as black women.

Leela not only lives better than Hattie Wilder, she lives better than other representations of black women characters struggling to survive on the land in black fiction. What she stands to lose also grants her a greater voice in defending her land against whites' greed. Unlike Sarah E. Wright's Mariah Upshur, who curses the white man in his absence, Leela confronts Wesley Sparks, the unscrupulous white bank teller who demands payment on $15,000 he lent T. J. to buy more acreage. Throwing her hat to the ground, Leela stands with arms akimbo, a bold posture of defiance against Sparks, who stole the money from the Mexia Community Bank, a lending institution that has denied loans to blacks. She questions and refuses Sparks's call for an immediate payback of the $3,000 balance. Her anger condemns Sparks's deliberate attempt to extort her land. She reminds him of his premeditated attempt to lend T. J. money for the land in order to repossess the property at his convenience.

Leela's racial "otherness" and gender difference provoke white aggression against her property. Her perceived inequality as a black female landowner spurs this aggression. But also, as a black female, Leela has fundamentally different economic interests in her land than the whites do. She grows melons on her farm; white males want oil gushers. A practical staple, the melons provide Leela with a comfortable standard of living while providing a food source for others. Conversely, gushers to her signify an impractical impoverishment of land; they rob the soil of vitality and cause farmers to lose their land and their sustenance. Reducing the crops that her husband tilled from cotton and corn to melons, Leela places herself in an agrarian African female tradition revealed to her through the childhood stories her Grandma Ekiti from Cameroon told her. As melon raiser, Leela engages in a test of sacrifice and ritual similar to the Cameroon women who work in melon fields. Whether to uproot the melons early during a drought or risk losing them by waiting for the rain in order to pay off Sparks is Leela's immediate predicament. She miscalculates the rains and loses the entire crop to a tornado.

Leela's setback fails to undermine her obstinacy in protecting her property rights. Determined that she will always reside at Rioluces, Leela engages in preemptive defense, to wrest the advantage of the first strike from her opponent.[8] Such a blow can be perceived as aggressive, even though defensive in nature. Leela uses preemptive defense against Sparks. She enlists a black male wildcatter, Victor Beaufort, to search for oil on her land. Oil discovery prompts southern racists to devise various strategies to seize Leela's land. Leela then rejects whites' offers to obtain a lease for ten dollars an acre and accepts Victor Beaufort's offer of one dollar an acre. Leela engages in a tit-for-tat combat with Sparks and southern racists as male aggression heightens. In each instance, whites retaliate. They steal Victor's shipment of drilling materials and torch Leela's oil fields. Fires and explosions symbolize the white mania and the southern white mind-set that black men and women should not be in the oil business.

What brings Leela and Victor together and, indeed, what holds the reader's interest in this historical romance is their desire to beat the system of white economic privilege. Both grew up in segregated Texas without economic security—Leela lived with her humble Aunt Effie, after losing both her parents and her grandmother to death as a child; Victor was an oil field orphan, cared for by a Cherokee woman. He wanted more out of life than twenty-five cents a day carrying buckets of water to men in the oil fields or two dollars a day digging ditches and laying pipe for whites. He wanted oil profits. With his brothers, he bought and restored rusted pipes and sold them to white companies. With the profits, he bought leases and made his own drilling supplies.

Leela, too, grew up with a fierce need for economic independence and a sense of control about her future as a black girl. As a teenager, it angered her to see Mr. Foreman, a local black newspaper owner she worked for, kowtow to city whites who dictated what he should print and threatened his business if he did not comply. His failure to print Leela's article about the need for sidewalks in the black community, because he feared what whites would do, also incurred her wrath. Leela's relationship with Mr. Foreman foreshadows the bond she has with Victor Beaufort. In both instances, she becomes a pawn in the racial game played out between greedy white men and bent-on-survival black men.

Leela's proximity to the racial war between the black male and white male racializes her social predicament and implicates gender structure already predetermined by social expectation. What society expects of her, however, differs from her perception of self. As a teenager, she took exception to Mr. Foreman firing her and telling her that she should be more concerned about finding a husband and starting a family than in interfering in men's affairs. Leela barks at the sexist-classist predicament that Mr. Foreman suggests for her. Women, to her thinking, should have more to look forward to than just getting married and having children. Leela voices her resistance to herself rather than to Mr. Foreman, but even so, her words become a defense lever to pry her from negative social expectations. She wants her independence first and a family second. What she wants for herself as a teenager conflicts with Mr. Foreman's definition of gender. Gender to him means oppositional roles for men and women based on their biological differences; this definition functions to remove Leela from the public arena of competing "men" to the private and less competitive site of motherhood.

Similarly, Victor Beaufort displaces Leela in contractual matters. He jeopardizes her female position as landowner by secretly signing a contract with Starr Oil to produce 750,000 barrels of oil a year on her property by having crude oil piped out of the ground and safely shipped to the refinery. His actions are driven by his fierce attempt to outsmart the white man, by male privilege he assumes in his romantic relationship with Leela, and by his inherent belief that the woman is not equal to the man when making decisions about land utilization. His failure to produce the required oil leads him to strike a deal with a dishonest third person, Carey Logan, Leela's brother-in-law, half-brother, and erstwhile lover, who forges leases to her land and sells them to whites. Each deal splits and transfers Leela's property to men and makes her gender struggle to keep her farm more difficult.

With the transfer of oil rights, Leela fights to preserve her class status. According to her thinking, her status as a landowner will protect her son's economic future. Believing that her son should receive his father's inheritance, she thrusts herself into Victor Beaufort's affairs regarding her land and offers suggestions about his wildcatting. She employs as much energy to save her land as the men use to wrestle it from her. In this dog-eat-dog boomtown, oil means money; money confers respectability to Leela as a stay-at-home widow.

Leela's class status links to her sexual attraction. What she owns makes her desirable—pretty clothes, a comfortable home, and oil-rich property. The same elements of class that contribute to her allure are what Victor admires and jeopardizes: full skirts over her curved hips, fringed lace on her shawl that dips into the fold between her breasts, the glowing fireside that warms her long shapely legs. The strength Leela possesses in her allure far exceeds Victor's ability to protect her assets. Each bad oil deal Victor engages in destabilizes Leela's wealth and threatens her class status.

In three confrontations with race, nineteen-year-old Leela pays a price for her assertiveness—she confronts the sheriff and then finds herself struggling to raise bail money for her cousin Parker; she opposes Mr. Foreman and then loses her job; and she stands up against Wesley Sparks and discovers her land under attack from oil speculators. Each confrontation represents a stage of growth. Together the three stages and Leela's growing pains symbolically represent gestational periods preceding birth. Her punishments come from her daring to go against the patriarchal system, but she gives birth to a stronger and more persistent self.

How she wants her life to be—a secure middle-class black woman landowner—conflicts with how it progresses. How it progresses originates with those in power positions. Her plight is typical of that of the female. Since men have traditionally created the means by which women engage their experiences, women, as sociologist Dorothy L. Smith suggests, must find a way to wrestle this power from a patriarchal mind-set.[9] Leela voices her rights and interrupts the male's pattern of gaining advantage through women's silence.

Leela's survival as a black middle-class woman is contingent on her ability to realize the kind of knowledge she needs to resist oppression. Her knowledge base consists of certain realities. She is black, female, and middle class—attributes that the majority population excludes from landownership. Consideration of these realities is necessary to resolve the problems others present to her as black woman landowner. Despite the devastation of her property, she must consider the historical climate that pits whites against blacks and blacks against each other. While her predicament with the larger society, with Victor, and with her various family members puts her in uncomfortable situations, she cannot let abstractions such as hatred, malice, and deceit cloud her decisions. She represents black women in complex relationships "where contextual rules," writes Patricia Hill Collins, "take priority over abstract principles in governing behavior."[10] Through discussions with her Aunt Effie, Leela works through her loss and Victor's role in it. Her eventual realization that Victor's pride has caused his decisions and that men think differently than women announces her birth into a higher realm of interpersonal communication. The man Leela has said she would never forgive, she admits she loves. The abstract principle of doing harm to others because they do harm to her is lost in Leela's reuniting with Victor. She sees in him the man she can rebuild her home with. Yet, in her acceptance of Victor, Leela maintains caution. She reminds Victor that he has brought to her considerable harm and that what he has done will not be easy for her to forget or forgive.

More than any other work of fiction in the African American literary canon, *Black Gold* offers a panoramic view of experiences that black women landowners share through the struggles and resistance of Leela Brannon Wilder. In her fight for autonomy through landownership, Leela opposes race, gender, and class prejudices. In her attempt to belong, she overcomes familial upsets. In her desire to love, she is exposed to and triumphs over crooks. A prototype in black fiction, Leela Wilder illuminates the historical gap between black women's attainment of property and society's belief in their difference and unworthiness as landowners. An American metaphor, Leela Brannon Wilder represents the black wife, mother, cousin, daughter-in-law, sister, and lover who dares to intrude into America's most patriarchal profit-taking enterprise—landownership.

Epilogue

From Reading Historical Romances to Expanding the African American Literary Canon

Reading African American women's historical romances should be more than a nonstop cursory perusal of a bygone era. It should be more than a titillating excursion into the affairs of colorful characters in on-again/off-again interludes. Reading historical romances should engage the more conscious activity of critically assessing black women activists in the text, realizing the need for their presence, and articulating the relevance of their presence to expanding the canon of African American literature.

Failure to assess militant heroines hinders full comprehension of the texts, resulting in an oversight of the narratives' mission and a myopic look at black female protagonists in these historical romances from 1989 to the present. As oppositional discourses, these narratives have as their main objective to counter and expand representations of black women in African American historical romances prior to 1989 and to offer a more expansive view of the resistance territory than previously recorded in African American literature. Deviating from fictional portrayals of nineteenth-century black women's traditional but peripheral involvement with such racist events as burnings and lynchings, black women appearing in more recent historical romances take center stage in resistance movements such as abolition, colonization, and westward expansion. Strong, wish-fulfilling, self-defining black heroines drive the content in these narratives as they target prevalent social biases and oppose the discrepancy between the rhetoric of American justice and the dispensation of injustice to African Americans. Their emotions, decisions, and ultimate responsibilities chart the progress of the narratives and their progress in the stories. They mix an ethical imperative to advance the race with a need to define themselves, thus illuminating a new dimension of black women in the black text.

Womanist protagonists in these historical romances are mobile figures, metaphors of change. Moving to sites of resistance, distant from the expected southern environment found in earlier black historical romances, self-defining protagonists make clear black women's persistent struggles for self-determination even in new territory. Their positions in this new locale parallel their new appearance in their public roles. No longer the mulatta evident in Harper's Iola Leroy, Hopkins's Mabelle Beaubean, or Frank Yerby's Desiree, protagonists in post-1989 historical romances have skin complexions ranging from caramel to sable. The presence of these darker-hued heroines gives a broader color spectrum of the race and a fuller view of African American women's contributions to nineteenth-century social reform.

Moreover, uncertainties of the new environment parallel complexities in the heroines' characters. These heroines are moral and immoral, wise and naive, giving and taking, accepting and critical. They make faux pas, bungle careers, walk away from marriage, and assume responsibility for other people's children. Human and lifelike, they differ from the cookie-cut, socially obedient nineteenth-century mulatta heroines. They bring to the freedom struggle individually designed tactics to combat biases erected against the racial group. Coming alive through their actions rather than through staid nineteenth-century narrative discourse, these heroines exist within an aesthetically subversive text which begins *in medias res,* closes open ended, reverses stereotypes, and interrupts the narrative with black cultural components.

The need for nineteenth-century black women activists in modern historical romances cannot be overestimated. These heroines offer a fuller portrait of black women who in nineteenth-century African American literature were often neglected, misrepresented, or abused. Black women activists in historical romances written by black women from 1989 to the present rectify three problems. First, their presence revises the neglect of darker-hued heroines in earlier novels, an omission based on the assumption that dark-hued female protagonists were inappropriate literary models to wage a fight against race/gender/class prejudices. The assumption is grounded in nineteenth-century accommodationist tactics and touted by African Americans who aspired to white ideals and white acceptance. The literature of the period mirrored near-white female protagonists with assimilationist ideals as tokens of acceptance. Late-twentieth-century historical romances rewrite racial politics to include darker-hued women and their ongoing participation in political struggles. Their appropriateness as literary models corresponds in kind to the prominence and relevance of dark-skinned Maria Stewart, Harriet Tubman, and Sojourner Truth, without whom race history would be considerably different.

Second, heroines in black women's late-twentieth-century historical romances dispel the myth that a husband's career should come before a wife's ambition. Marriage for these heroines fails to halt the activists' participation in community uplift. Rivaling the husband's career and ignoring his demands, as does Sable Fontaine in *Through the Storm*, heroines in the post-1989 narratives take a tougher stance than do heroines in nineteenth-century novels such as Iola Leroy, who queries her husband about whether she should enter the job market. Moreover, womanist heroines in post-1989 historical romances seem to expand their ambition for freedom by giving birth to female children. Unlike heroines in nineteenth-century novels whose lives end with marriage, women in recent historical romances extend their mission during marriage by creating in their image another brood of freedom fighters. What these later heroines suggest is that marriage does not and should not prevent black women from carrying out their mission of resistance.

Third, black women activists in these post-1989 historical romances satisfy a moral imperative. Duty-bound to uplift the race, they fulfill a salient requirement for nineteenth-century black womanhood. They document black women's presence in and contributions to specific moments of history, heretofore ignored or given little notice in black literature. Recapturing the bygone era of the abolitionist movement, the colonization movement, the Exodusters movement, and Mexia's oil boom, these narratives establish black women in nineteenth-century and early-twentieth-century public roles and track oppressive biases they contend with. Their militant roles in specific historical moments replace the victims of slavery and Reconstruction rehearsed in nineteenth-century historical romances.

Black women's militant presence in late-twentieth-century historical romances has obvious relevance to the expansion of the African American literary canon. Their militant existence in these female-centered narratives augments the literary canon that has reserved the role of social reformer primarily to the black male. These heroines correct the misconception given by nineteenth-century fiction that black women had little or no input in the freedom struggles and that their public aspirations should have been subordinated to their private responsibilities. Their participation in these late-twentieth-century narratives about nineteenth-century life expands the canon to a broader perspective of African American social history and black women's inclusion in that history.

Then, too, these heroines appear in narratives that avoid the familiar South-to-North trek of Iola Leroy and Mabelle Beaubean; they embark on an East-to-West, South-to-West, or North-to-West journey. This larger geographical trek parallels their personal migration from unfulfilled desire to desire fulfilled. Overcoming race, gender, and class victimization, these heroines metaphorically progress through the triple stages of insemination (desire), pregnancy (social gestation), and birth (self-fulfillment and identity), while advancing the notion that the home is the primary site for gender empowerment and subversion. The travel and home motifs reconstruct gender duality and identity and contest the assumption borne by nineteenth-century literature that black women were reductive, traditional, nonpolitical minitravelers.

African American women's historical romances written from 1989 to the present will be valued for their expansion of the African American literary canon, whose viability is only as good as its capacity to grow and develop. An expanded canon is needed to accommodate a changing fiction—one that challenges a patriarchal history and social order and that provides for the inclusion of womanist agents for social reform. The heroines of black women's recent historical romances are such agents. Their struggles with race, gender, sexuality, and class, their embracing an African-centered culture, and their appearance in subversive narratives present an expanded view of black women activists in popular late-twentieth-century historical romances too long overlooked. To ignore these novels is to jeopardize territorial expansion sorely needed in the African American literature canon.

Notes

Introduction: Reading African American Women's Historical Romances

1. Patricia Hill Collins, *Black Feminist Thought: Knowledge, Consciousness, and the Politics of Empowerment* (New York: Routledge, 1991), 4.
2. Maria W. Stewart, *Maria W. Stewart: America's First Black Woman Political Writer: Essays and Speeches.* Ed. Marilyn Richardson (Bloomington and Indianapolis: Indiana UP, 1987), 53.
3. George Dekker, *The American Historical Romance* (Cambridge and New York: Cambridge UP, 1987), 4.
4. Nikki Giovanni shows no interest in man-woman narratives and would avoid reading historical romances. She believes the man-woman relationship offers the woman too few options: Either she disrobes or she does not. See Claudia Tate's interview of Nikki Giovanni in *Black Women Writers at Work* (New York: Continuum, 1983), 66.
5. M. Giulia Fabi, *Passing and the Rise of the African American Novel* (Chicago: U of Chicago P, 2001), 107.
6. Irons's argument can be applied to the exclusion of African American literature from white American literature before academia expanded its definition of American literature to include ethnic literatures. The same argument can be applied to black women's literature long deprecated in literary circles by white and black males before these critics, often grudgingly, expanded the canon to recognize gender studies. And the argument holds true for black historical romances ignored by black feminist scholars, many of whom have not crossed the bridge to black popular readings. Thus, the cycle of exclusion repeats itself, dis-

rupting the continuity of African American literature rather than preserving its territorial integrity. See Glenwood Irons, *Gender, Language and Myth: Essays on Popular Narrative* (Toronto: U of Toronto P, 1992), xiii.

7. Anita Richmond Bunkley is an Ohio native and the daughter of writer Virginia L. Richmond. A magna cum laude graduate of Mount Union College in Alliance, Ohio, Bunkley moved with her two daughters to Houston, Texas, in 1980, where she married Crawford Bunkley III in 1986 and became director of volunteers for the American Red Cross. She is unique among African American historical romance novelists in that her oeuvre is Texas based. Bunkley made her debut in romance fiction with the self-published *Emily, the Yellow Rose* in 1989. Other romances soon followed: *Black Gold* (1994), *Wild Embers* (1996), *Starlight Passage* (1997), and *Balancing Act* (1998). These stories fulfill Bunkley's childhood dream to write about African American women "who lived, loved, and triumphed in important periods of time." Her other works include the nonfiction *Steppin' Out with Attitude: Sister, Sell Your Dream* (1998) and two anthologies: *Sisters* (1996) and *Girlfriends* (1999), which she edited with Eva Rutland and Sandra Kitt and in which she has two short stories. To date, Bunkley has more than 400,000 copies of her works in print. She is well represented on the Internet at www.rinard.com/arbunkley or www.anitabunkley.com. Accessed May 14, 2003.
8. Beverly Jenkins (née Hunter), a Detroit native and lay preacher who writes under her married name, gained from her mother an appreciation of history, especially of the black experience, which textbooks in the public schools she attended virtually ignored. Lamenting the fact that few people knew anything about black history during the period between the end of slavery and the Civil Rights movement, Jenkins says, "History books have a tendency to say we didn't exist. . . . It's always black folks come to America, black folks were slaves, black folks were freed in 1865. Then we disappeared. History picks us up again rioting in Watts in 1965. But what happened for those 100 years?" Jenkins answers her own question in her historical romances, for which she has done extensive research and in which she dramatizes race, gender, and class oppression in the lives of black women and men. Her primary focus in these novels, though, is on how the black woman forged a public career and expressed her total self despite race, gender, and class prejudice. Jenkins's ten historical romances to date are *Night Song* (1994), *Vivid* (1995), *Indigo* (1996), *Topaz* (1997), *Through the Storm* (1998), *The Taming of Jessie Rose* (1990), *Always and Forever* (2000), *Before the Dawn* (2001), *Belle and Beau* (2002), and *A Chance at Love* (2002). See Ed Decker, "Beverly Jenkins," *Contemporary Black Biography*, ed. Mpho L. Mabunde and Shirelle Phelps, vol. 14 (Detroit: Gale Research 1997), 139.
9. Shirley Hailstock is from Columbia, South Carolina, and is currently a teacher in New Jersey. She has published only one historical romance, *Clara's Promise* (1995), which won her the Utah Romance Writers Heart of the West Award. Primarily a writer of mainstream women's fiction, Hailstock nevertheless offers advice to the novice who wants to write the ethnic historical romance, especially the African American historical romance. She suggests that one include background, traditions, taboos, methods of speech and expression, descriptions of physical attributes, occupation, and setting. She believes that "books written by African American . . . women [who use the aforementioned characteristics in their historical romances] will bring them a new perspective to the genre." Hailstock's mainstream works include *Whispers of Love* (1994), *White Diamonds* (1996), *Legacy* (1997), and *More than Gold* (2000). Her webpage is at www.geocities.com/Paris/Bistro/6812; accessed May 14, 2003 (Hailstock interview with Dandridge, 7 Dec. 2000).
10. Francine Craft is a native of Mississippi and formerly a resident of New Orleans, the setting for her first and only historical novel, *The Black Pearl* (1996). A retired District of Columbia

government worker, Craft has also worked as an elementary school teacher and research assistant for a nonprofit organization. A modern romance writer, she has published seven novels: *Devoted* (1995), *Lyrics of Love* (1998), *Still in Love* (1999), *Star Crossed* (2000), *Betrayed by Love* (2000), *Forever Love* (2001), and *What Matters Most* (2002). Her short stories "Misty's Mothers" and "A Love Made in Heaven" have been anthologized in *A Mother's Love* (1996), ed. Monica Harris, and in *Wedding Bells* (1999), ed. Gwynne Forster, Francine Craft, and Niqui Stanhope.

11. Gay G. Gunn is a Washington, D.C., native, the oldest of three children and a graduate of Howard University, with a B.A. in sociology and an M.A. in social work. She is married with two adult sons. Her careers have included social work in the Washington, D.C., court system, academic advising at American University, guidance director at a parochial high school in Washington, D.C., journalist contributing to the monthly column "Personal Reflections" in *Washington Living Magazine*, and novelist. As novelist, Ms. Gunn has published two romances, *Everlastin' Love* (1996) and *Pride and Joi* (2002), and one historical romance, *Nowhere to Run* (1997), under the imprint of Genesis Press in Columbus, Mississippi. Each tells the story of strong black characters who remain committed to their goals. "That's what I want to celebrate," writes Gunn, "the possibility of us as a people. It doesn't always have to be about us living rural poor or urban ghetto. It doesn't always have to be about the struggle and tragedy of Black Life. Our lives are complex." See Gwen Osborne, "Gay G. Gunn," *Romantic Times*, 20 April 1999.
12. Smith's valuable essay is one of the oldest to lay the foundation for black "feminist" scholarship. Seizing an opportunity to theorize black women's experiences, she uses terminology employed by white feminist critics. See Barbara Smith, "Toward a Black Feminist Criticism," in *But Some of Us Are Brave*, ed. Gloria T. Hull, Patricia Bell Scott, and Barbara Smith (Old Westbury, NY: Feminist P, 1982), 159.
13. Thomas Jefferson, *Notes on the State of Virginia*, ed. William Peden (Chapel Hill: U of North Carolina P, 1955), 138.
14. Evelyn Higginbotham, "African American Women's History and the Metalanguage of Race," *Signs: Journal of Women in Culture and Society* 17 (Winter 1992): 256.
15. In 1994, Frances Smith Foster anthologized and reprinted Harper's first three historical romances, *Minnie's Sacrifice, Sowing and Reaping,* and *Trial and Triumph,* under the Beacon imprint.
16. Frances Harper, *Iola Leroy, or Shadows Uplifted* (1892; reprint, New York: AMS, 1971), 282.
17. Pauline Hopkins, *Contending Forces: A Romance Illustrative of Negro Life in the South* (1900; reprint, New York: AMS, 1971), 13.
18. In fact, Jenkins says, "My mission in life has turned into bringing [black] history back to life. . . . We are a very, very proud race"; quoted in Mabunde and Phelps, *Contemporary Black Biography*, 138. See Barbara Christian, *Black Women Novelists: The Development of a Tradition, 1892–1976* (Westport, CT: Greenwood Press, 1980), 28.
19. Higginbotham, "Metalanguage of Race," 254.
20. See descriptions of black women in Winthrop D. Jordan, *White over Black: American Attitudes toward the Negro, 1550–1812* (New York: Norton, 1977), 34–35, based on historical records culled from the South.
21. Teresa de Lauretis, *Technologies of Gender: Essays on Theory, Film, and Fiction* (Bloomington: Indiana UP, 1987), 5.
22. Slave narratives expose the difficulty that black men and women had in establishing a viable romantic relationship owing to the indecency of slave masters. Henry Bibb writes in

his narrative, "There is no legal marriage among the slaves in the South; I never saw nor heard of such a thing in my life. . . . A slave marriage according to the law is a thing unknown in the history of American slavery. . . . Licentious white men can, and do, enter at night or day the lodging places of slaves; break the bonds of affection in families; destroy all their domestic and social union for life; and the laws of the country afford them no protection." See "Narrative of the Life of Henry Bibb" (1817) in *Puttin' on Ole Massa*, ed. Gilbert Osofsky (New York: Harper and Row, 1969), 77–78. Moses Gandy, whose first wife was sold from him and who could not see his second wife, argues in his narrative, "No colored man wishes to live at the house where his wife lives, for he has to endure the continual misery of seeing her flogged or abused, without daring to say a word in her defence." See *Narrative of the Life of Moses Gandy, Late a Slave* (Boston: Oliver Johnson, 1844), 16.

23. Rather than make Jacks's letter the focal point of the conference, Ruffin defended all women against Jacks's allegations of ignorance and immorality and made clear that the women's club movement was not created solely for upper-class women but also for all black women, including those teaching in the South and their mothers who were unable to obtain schooling. See Elizabeth L. Davis, *Lifting as They Climb: African American Women Writers, 1910–1940* (New York: G. K. Hall, 1995), 14, 18.

24. Frank Garvin Yerby (1916–1991) was a prolific African American writer of historical romances. Setting his stories in the antebellum South, he depicted whites as his major characters and stereotyped young mulattas as voluptuous mistresses of white males. In Yerby's first novel, *The Foxes of Harrow* (1946), sixteen-year-old Desiree Hippolyte becomes the mulatta concubine of Stephen Harrow, the wealthy, married white protagonist.

25. Benjamin Quarles, *Black Abolitionists* (New York: Oxford UP, 1969), 178. The pre–Civil War cases of Jarena Lee and Maria Stewart are legendary. Jarena Lee's ordination to preach in the A.M.E. Church was delayed eight years by Bishop Richard Allen, who had founded the A.M.E. Church because of the racial injustices he perceived in the white church; he had been relegated as a black to the balcony and restricted to a specific time for prayer at the communion table. And Maria Stewart publicly alluded to the sexism of patriarchal men of color: "I am sensible that there are many highly intelligent gentlemen of color in these United States, in the force of whose arguments, doubtless, I shall discover my inferiority; but if they are blest with wit and talent . . . why have they not made themselves men of eminence, by . . . endeavoring to alleviate the woes of their brethren in bondage?" See Jarena Lee, "The Life and Religious Experiences of Jarena Lee: A Colored Lady Giving an Account of Her Call to Preach the Gospel," in Dorothy Porter, ed., *Early Negro Writing, 1760–1837* (Boston: Beacon, 1971), 494–514; and Bert Loewenberg and Ruth Bogin, *Black Women in Nineteenth-Century American Life: Their Works, Their Thoughts, Their Feelings* (University Park: Pennsylvania State UP, 1976), 196.

26. Belinda Hurmence, ed., *Before Freedom: 48 Oral Histories of Former North and South Carolina Slaves* (New York: Mentor, 1990), 192.

27. Eugene D. Genovese, *Roll, Jordan, Roll: The World the Slaves Made* (New York: Pantheon, 1974), 431.

28. I am indebted to Clenora Hudson-Weems for the term "Africana womanism," which she coined in 1987 to lay the groundwork for reassessing the black woman activist's identity. See Clenora Hudson-Weems, *Africana Womanism: Reclaiming Ourselves* (Troy, MI: Bedford, 1993), 22–23.

29. Ibid., 55–73.

30. For a discussion of the aesthetic value of female-centered texts that engage in principles of

narrative desire, see Claudia Tate, *Domestic Allegories of Political Desire* (New York: Oxford UP, 1992), 8.

31. Patricia Hill Collins in *Black Feminist Thought* and Barbara Smith in her essay "Toward a Black Feminist Criticism" couch African American women's experiences in a theoretical framework under the title of "feminism." This terminology was first used to describe the assertive experiences of white middle-class women, not of black women. Notwithstanding the historical disconnect between mainstream feminists and the Africana womanist, black feminist scholars occasionally attach the feminist label to womanist ideology. In this study, I incorporate the prevailing attitudes of feminists only when they correspond with and enhance the emancipatory ideology of black womanism.

32. According to Phyllis Schlafly, founder of Stop ERA, one of the negative aspects of the women's liberation movement was that feminists told women, "The home is a cage or a prison from which women must be liberated." Quoted in Katheryn Cullen-Dupont, ed., *American Women Activists' Writings: An Anthology 1637–2002* (New York: Cooper Square, 2002), 512.

33. Feminism, as a concept, is problematic to the historical reality of the Africana womanist, who, unlike her white activist counterpart, has worked with her mate for racial uplift and social betterment. Moreover, the term *feminism* suggests a natural alignment of black and white women in mutual causes that simply did not exist. White women, for instance, have historically excluded Africana women from their organizations that have purported to serve and benefit African Americans. Among the abolitionists, white women who abhorred slavery debated whether black women should join their ranks in abolitionist societies. Because of race prejudice, black women were sparsely represented at the National Convention of Female Anti-Slavery Societies and in the chapters of antislavery societies in various cities. Throughout the nineteenth century, black women were rebuffed in temperance groups and at the General Federation of Women's Clubs which white feminists organized. Shunned at the General Federation in 1900, Josephine St. Pierre Ruffin appealed to colored women to "confine themselves to their clubs and the large field of work there." See Sharon Harley and Rosalyn Terborg-Penn, eds., *The Afro-American Woman: Struggles and Images* (Baltimore: Black Classic Press, 1978), 17–27.

34. Quoted in Loewenberg and Bogin, *Black Women in Nineteenth-Century American Life*, 235.

35. Anna Julia Cooper, *A Voice from the South.* (1892; reprint, New York: Oxford UP, 1988), 134.

36. Power for the supposedly "weaker" sex is used to effect personal and communal accomplishments, not to demand others' submission. Bernice Carroll in "Peace Research: The Cult of Power" categorizes powers of the powerless as follows: (1) disintegrative power, (2) inertia power, (3) innovative and norm-creating power, (4) legitimizing power, (5) expressive power, (6) explosive power, (7) power of resistance, (8) collective power, and (9) migratory power. *Journal of Conflict Resolution* 16.4 (1972), 608–09.

37. Ibid., 613–14.

38. Elmer P. Martin and Joanne Mitchell Martin, *Social Work and the Black Experience* (Washington, DC: National Association of Social Workers, 1995), 2.

39. Thomas A. Parham, Joseph L. White, and Adisa Ajamu, *The Psychology of Blacks: An African-Centered Perspective* (Upper Saddle River, NJ: Prentice Hall, 1999), 14.

40. Peter Brooks, *Reading for the Plot: Design and Intention in Narrative* (New York: Alfred A. Knopf, 1984), 6.

41. These five writers do not represent all of the post-1989 black historical romance writers, but I have chosen them because their works best represent the theme of resistance that this study is trying to project. Roberta Gayle, Patricia Vaughn, and Mildred Riley are other black women writers of historical romances. To my knowledge, only one African American woman has written an historical romance with all white characters. That person is Francis Ray, who wrote *The Bargain* (1995). The novel introduces heiress Alexander Carstairs in a romance with Thorne Blakemore, the fifth Earl of Grayson in England in 1859.

Chapter 1: Antebellum Activism: The Call to Freedom

1. Maria W. Stewart, "Lecture Delivered at the Franklin Hall," in *Maria W. Stewart, America's First Black Woman Political Writer: Essays and Speeches,* ed. Marilyn Richardson (Bloomington and Indianapolis: Indiana UP, 1987), 45.
2. See Benjamin Quarles, *The Negro in the Making of America* (New York: Collier, 1969), 95.
3. Seven years after completing *Emily, the Yellow Rose,* Bunkley still did not have a publisher. She had received 32 rejections from publishers who doubted whether white America could enjoy a black love story. She and her second husband, Crawford Bunkley III, a senior public affairs representative with Exxon in Houston, used their family savings to found Rinard Press. They published 11,000 copies of this novel. *Emily, the Yellow Rose* shares a similar publishing history with its nineteenth-century cousins, *Iola Leroy* and *Contending Forces.* Kept from mainstream publishers because of racial restrictions, Harper published *Iola Leroy* under the imprint of the Colored Cooperative, a small publishing company in Boston, Massachusetts; Pauline Hopkins used the family press that she started with her savings to publish *Contending Forces.* See Paul Harasim, "Bunkley's Debut an Inspiration," *Houston Chronicle,* 30 Oct. 1989: A13, and Barbara Karkabi's "Desire, Discipline, Drive," *Houston Chronicle,* 9 Nov. 1998: C1, C3.
4. See Randolph B. Campbell, *An Empire for Slavery: The Peculiar Institution in Texas: 1821–1865* (Baton Rouge: Louisiana State UP 1989), 16.
5. In 1821, Stephen F. Austin inherited a land grant that had been given to his recently deceased father Moses Austin to settle an Anglo-American community at San Felipe de Austin, in southeastern Texas, near Houston. During the war between Anglos and Mexicans, San Felipe de Austin was the site of the 1832 and 1833 republican conventions and also served as capital of the provisional government in 1835. The following year, the town was evacuated and burned to keep it out of the hands of the Mexican Army. Incorporated in 1837, San Felipe de Austin became the seat of Austin County. See "San Felipe de Austin, Texas," *Handbook of Texas Online,* at http://www.tsha.utexas.edu/handbook/online/articles/view/SS/hls10.html. Accessed 14 May 2003.
6. Washington on the Brazos, also known as Old Washington, was established in 1814 and had a prominent political history. Located above the Brazos River in the upper northeast of Washington County, the town served as headquarters for General Sam Houston's army and then as the capital of the Texas Republic from 1842 to 1846. See "Washington," *Texas Online,* at http://www.texas-on-line.com/graphic/washngtn.htm. Accessed 7 May 2003.
7. Campbell, *An Empire for Slavery,* 24.
8. Ibid.
9. The Anglos declared their own republic when the Mexican Congress instituted what white

settlers considered oppressive laws—two of the more intolerable were taxation on imports and the cessation of immigration.

10. Benjamin Lundy (1789–1839), a New Jersey native and Quaker, went to Texas in 1830, 1833, and 1834 to find a suitable location to establish a colony for blacks. During most of the trips, he walked for miles in the hottest weather and was often afflicted with cholera, for which he medicated himself with camphor and laudanum. His labors were arduous and his trips difficult, but he was convinced that "the sufferings of the slave were greater than [his] own." Lundy's plan to colonize free blacks in Texas failed to materialize. He was unable to appeal a law of April 6, 1830, expressly prohibiting United States citizens from emigrating to Texas, and in 1834 the Mexican legislature decided to enact a law prohibiting the further issuing of land grants for settlement. See Schoen, "The Free Negro in the Republic of Texas," *Southwestern Quarterly* 39 (April 1936): 303; Benjamin Lundy, *The Life, Travels and Opinions of Benjamin Lundy, Including His Journeys to Texas and Mexico; with a Sketch of Contemporary Events, and a Notice of the Revolution in Hayti.* 1847. New York: Negro Universities P, 1969. The quotation is taken from p. 31.
11. According to Benjamin Lundy, the Mexican government issued Nicholas Drouett a grant to colonize colored Louisianians. See Lundy, 113; Schoen, 305.
12. Schoen, 307.
13. Schoen, 301–2.
14. In the novel, the anonymous ballad precedes the preface, and Joshua Kinney, a free Creek medicine man and Emily's lover, sings the song originally composed by an anonymous slave. Over the years, various transcriptions of the ballad have appeared, including those of Texas composer David W. Guion and television maestro Mitch Miller. A boogie-woogie transcription of the song appeared in 1956 which completely altered the words of the original Negro folk song. For further explanation of these transcriptions, see Martha Anne Turner, *The Yellow Rose of Texas: Her Saga and Her Song with the Santa Anna Legend* (Austin: Shoal Creek Publishers, 1976), 67–78, 87–92, and 93–95.
15. For an insightful overview of details, see the chapter "Santa Anna and the Slave Girl at San Jacinto" in Turner, 5–39.
16. See Stephen Harrigan, "The Yellow Rose of Texas," *Texas Monthly* 12 (April 1984): 152.
17. James Morgan (1787–1866), a Philadelphia native and Texas pioneer, became an agent for the New Washington Association in 1835. For this company, he purchased land, later known as Morgan Point, at the mouth of the San Jacinto River. The company then brought to Texas free blacks, among whom was Emily D. West. See B. R. Brunson and Andrew Forest Muir, "Morgan, James," *Handbook of Texas Online*, at http://www.tsha.utexas.edu/handbook/online/articles/view/ MM/fm050.html. Accessed 14 May 2003.
18. David A. Williams, *Bricks without Straw: A Comprehensive History of African Americans in Texas* (Austin: Eakin, 1997), 18.
19. See Margaret Swett Henson, "She's the Real Thing," *Texas Highways* 33.4 (April 1986): 60–61.
20. Campbell, *An Empire for Slavery*, 43.
21. Ibid., footnote 13.
22. Clarence Ray Wharton, *Wharton's History of Fort Bend County* (San Antonio: The Naylor Co., 1939), 11–12.
23. See Paul Ricoeur, *Time and Narrative* (Chicago: U of Chicago P, 1984), vol. 1, chapters 4–6; Wallace Martin, *Recent Theories of Narrative* (Ithaca, NY: Cornell UP, 1986), 76.

24. James Oliver Horton estimates that free blacks represented 10 percent of the population in the 1830s. Based on Eugene Genovese's analysis of the percentage increase of free blacks from 1790 to 1830, I conclude that free blacks numbered approximately 389,195 in the 1830s. See James Oliver Horton's *Free People of Color: Inside the African American Community* (Washington, DC: Smithsonian Institution P, 1993), 2; and Eugene D. Genovese, *Roll, Jordan Roll: The World the Slaves Made* (New York: Pantheon, 1974), 400.
25. Schoen, "The Free Negro in the Republic of Texas," 302.
26. John Reese is the fictional representative for John Reed, one of James Morgan's business partners. See Feris A. Bass, Jr., and B. R. Brunson, eds., *Fragile Empires: The Texas Correspondence of Samuel Swartwout and James Morgan, 1836–1856* (Austin: Shoal Creek, 1978).
27. Tracey E. Ore, ed., *The Social Construction of Difference and Inequality: Race, Class, Gender, and Sexuality* (Mountain View, CA: Mayfield, 2000), 207.
28. Christa Reiser, *Reflections on Anger: Women and Men in a Changing Society* (Westport, CT: Praeger, 1999).
29. On December 22, 1834, James Morgan, acting as agent for the New Washington Company, bought 1,600 acres of land from Joseph C. Clopper for $3,200. Here he founded the New Washington colony located on the northwest end of Galveston Bay. Only a few buildings and warehouses were constructed on this land before the Mexicans decimated the settlement in April 1836, just before the Battle of San Jacinto. New Washington is now known as Morgan's Point. See June A. Begeman, "Lynchburg, Cedar Bayou and Morgan's Point Ferryboats: Historical Highlights," *Touchstone* 7 (1988): 10.
30. Orange Grove became the name that James Morgan, in real life, gave to the residence he rebuilt after the Mexicans destroyed the old homestead in April 1836.
31. The character Diana suggests Diana Leonard, one of the free black women who migrated to Texas in 1835 and who worked for one year in the household of Colonel James Morgan. She survived the Mexican attack on Morgan's plantation and went to live in Houston, where she provided for herself and her small child on her earnings as a washerwoman. See Harold Schoen, "The Free Negro in the Republic of Texas," *Southwestern Historical Quarterly* 39 (April 1936): 302.
32. In the Mexican social hierarchy, woman was man's inferior. In fact, Mexican historians who place Emily at the Battle of San Jacinto refer to her as Santa Anna's "quadroon mistress" rather than as his "captive slave girl." The former reference gives the more favorable reputation to Santa Anna, Mexico's national hero, than to the beautiful women who attached themselves to him. See Martha Anne Turner, *The Yellow Rose of Texas*, 99.
33. Harrigan argues that Emily was a subsidiary feature of Sam Houston's victory and that General Santa Anna's libido and bad judgment led to his defeat. "Why," asks Harrigan, "did Santa Anna choose an untenable encampment on the plains of San Jacinto with the Texas Army in front of him and a bayou prohibiting his retreat?" The answer is that Santa Anna wanted to have immediate sex with Emily, his recent captive. See Stephen Harrigan, "The Yellow Rose of Texas," *Texas Monthly* 12 (April 1984): 152.
34. For a fuller description of Santa Anna's attitude toward Sam Houston's army, see Turner, *The Yellow Rose of Texas*, 19.
35. Harrigan, "The Yellow Rose of Texas."
36. Sue Bailey Thurman, *Pioneers of Negro Origin in California* (San Francisco: Acme, 1952), 47.

37. John William Templeton, *Our Roots Run Deep: The Black Experience in California*, vol. 1, *1500–1900* (San Jose, CA: Electron Access Inc., 1997), 233.
38. "'Mammy' Pleasant: Memoirs and Autobiography," *The Pandex of the Press* 1 (January 1902), 4.
39. See Florence H. Pettit, *America's Indigo Blues: Resist-printed and Dyed Textiles of the Eighteenth Century* (New York: Hastings House, 1974), 26, 39–40.
40. Harriet Tubman (1821–1913) was a Maryland fugitive named Araminta at birth and an ardent supporter of abolitionism. Regarding her mission as philanthropic and humanitarian, Tubman used the meager earnings from her domestic work to rescue her family members from slavery and to travel to the South approximately 19 times to aid the escape of more than 200 slaves. Tubman was undaunted by the Fugitive Slave Law of 1850 and by the $40,000 reward for her capture. Historically known as "Black Moses," she continued her Underground Railroad rescue missions until 1860, and it is said that she never lost a slave in her charge. For further details of Tubman's life, see Darlene Clark Hine, ed., *Black Women in America: An Historical Encyclopedia*, vol. 2 (Brooklyn, NY: Carlson, 1993), 1177; and Anne Parrish, *A Clouded Star* (New York: Harper, 1948), 96, 101.
41. Henrietta Buckmaster, *Let My People Go: The Story of the Underground Railroad and the Growth of the Abolitionist Movement* (1941; reprinted, Columbia: U of South Carolina P, 1993), xiv.
42. Indigo seeds were first introduced into South Carolina in 1740 when the Governor of Antigua sent them to his daughter, Eliza Lucas, who planted them and produced a successful crop. Charleston exported 100,000 pounds to England the following year and by 1747 had a monopoly on the product and began its manufacture to obtain a deep violet blue dye. The process for obtaining the dye was laborious, troublesome, and eventually unhealthy, yet the indigo dye at the time was the most effective coloring material. Many planters doubled their investment in several years, but by 1850, when cotton increased in value, indigo vanished from Charleston's list of exports. See Pettit, *America's Indigo Blues*, 26, 39–40.
43. James H. Dormon, ed., *Creoles of Color of the Gulf South* (Knoxville: U of Tennessee P, 1996), 5.
44. Historian James H. Dormon writes: "A few [colored Creoles] felt compassion for those in bondage, especially slaves who might be related by blood or marriage, but most considered their blacks principally as chattel properties. They bought, sold, mortgaged, willed, traded, and transferred their slaves, demanded long hours in the workshops and fields, and disciplined recalcitrant blacks." See *Creoles of Color of the Gulf South*, 54–55.

Chapter Two: Civil War Volunteerism: The Call to Reconstitute Family

1. Despite the variously composed black slave kinship groups, Herbert G. Gutman argues that the stable family was prevalent in the Deep South. See Gutman, *The Black Family in Slavery and Freedom, 1750–1925* (New York: Pantheon, 1976), 275.
2. In contrast to Herbert Gutman's view of the two-parent black family, Brenda E. Stevenson, in her study of Virginia, argues that the flexible extended family was more of the norm in

Virginia. See Stevenson, *Life in Black and White: Family and Community in the Slave South* (New York: Oxford UP, 1996), 256.

3. Darlene Clark Hine and Kathleen Thompson, *A Shining Thread of Hope: The History of Black Women in America* (New York: Broadway Books, 1998), 86.
4. C. Peter Ripley, *Slaves and Freedmen in Civil War Louisiana* (Baton Rouge: Louisiana State UP, 1976), 376.
5. Peter Bardaglio, "The Children of Jubilee: African American Childhood in Wartime," in Catherine Clinton and Nina Silber, eds., *Divided Houses: Gender and the Civil War* (New York: Oxford UP, 1992), 226.
6. Katherine M. Franke, "Taking Care," *Chicago-Kent Law Review* 76 (2001), 1548.
7. Patricia Hill Collins, *Black Feminist Thought: Knowledge, Consciousness, and the Politics of Empowerment* (New York: Routledge, 1991), 119.
8. American Freedmen's Inquiry Commission, St. Louis, Mo., November and December 1863, RG 94, M619, Roll 201 at 84, National Archives.
9. Jeanne L. Noble, *Beautiful, Also, Are the Souls of My Black Sisters: A History of the Black Woman in America* (Englewood Cliffs, NJ: Prentice-Hall, 1978), 28.
10. See Luce Irigaray, *This Sex Which Is Not One*, trans. from the French by Catherine Porter with Carolyn Burke (Ithaca: Cornell UP, 1985), 209.
11. Patricia Yaeger, *Honey-Mad Women: Emancipatory Strategies in Women's Writing* (New York: Columbia UP, 1988), 5.
12. Ed Decker, "Beverly Jenkins," in Mpho L. Mabunde and Shirelle Phelps, eds., *Contemporary Black Biography*, vol. 14 (Detroit: Gale Research, 1997), 139.

Chapter Three: Postbellum Activism: The Call to Heal

1. Thomsonianism was named after Samuel Thomson (1769–1843), a well-known herbalist who also utilized the vapor bath. See Gert H. Brieger, ed., *Medical America in the Nineteenth Century: Readings from the Literature* (Baltimore: Johns Hopkins P, 1972), 139; and John Duffy, *The Healers: A History of American Medicine* (Urbana: U of Illinois P, 1979), 110–14.
2. The Eclectic school, founded by Wooster Beach (1794–1859), employed both herbal and mineral remedies. See Duffy, *The Healers*, 114–15.
3. Homeopaths advocated limited drug use and disease prevention with personal cleanliness, appropriate diet, and clean air and water. For background and a fuller description of the basic principles of homeopathy in the United States, see Duffy, *The Healers*, 112–14, 115–18.
4. Hydropathy became a formal medical treatment in America around 1840. It was a method of administering to the ill by bathing the patient internally and externally with pure or mineral water. Duffy, *The Healers*, 121.
5. Historian Marita Graham Goodson mentions in passing that Dr. Francis Peyre Porcher, an 1847 graduate of Charleston's medical school, utilized the medical information he had obtained from Santee, South Carolina, slaves to publish his thesis, *A Medico-Botanical Catalogue of the Plants and Ferns of St. John's Berkeley, South Carolina*. I concur with Goodson's statement and offer several reasons that have led me to this conclusion, even though Dr. Porcher's biographer Dr. Jonathan M. Townsend attributes to Porcher's collection of botanical data the analytical mind of his French ancestry. First, time did not allow

Dr. Porcher, with his thriving medical practice, to wade through swamps, woods, and fields in an arduous and solitary search for herbs. Second, by his own admission, Dr. Porcher engaged in his botanical studies at a time when "it was rather regarded as a reproach for the educated physician to be at all addicted to botanical investigation." Third, that he had more than a small interest in the herbs that blacks collected is known from his knowledge that blacks gathered their herbs with full leaves. In mentioning his "general descriptions for collecting and drying medicinal substances of the vegetable kingdom," Dr. Porcher, instead of acknowledging blacks' contributions to his understanding of herbs and roots, stereotypes those who collect and import plants with full leaves as "savages" or "ignorant persons." He believed that the full leaf was the only way the "ignorant" gatherer could identify the plant. See Marita Graham Goodson, "Medical-Botanical Contributions of African Slave Women to American Medicine," in Darlene Clark Hine, ed., *Black Women in United States History* (New York: Carlson Press, 1990), vol. 2, 475; J. Townsend, "Francis Peyre Porcher," *Annals of Medical History,* Third Series, 1939: I, 177; and Francis Peyre Porcher, *Resources of the Southern Fields and Forests, Medical, Economical, and Agricultural*... (Charleston: Steam-Power Press/Evans and Cogswell, 1863).

6. Statistics reveal that in 1890, only 115 black women physicians and surgeons existed compared with 794 black male physicians. See Department of Commerce, Bureau of the Census, *Negro Population in the United States, 1790–1915* (1918; reprint, New York: Arno Press, 1968).
7. Darlene Clark Hine, "Co-Laborers in the Work of the Lord: Nineteenth-Century Black Women Physicians," in Hine, ed., *Black Women in United States History,* 638.
8. See F. Campbell Stewart, "The Actual Condition of the Medical Profession in This Country; with a Brief Account of Some of the Causes Which Tend to Impede Its Progress and Interfere with Its Honors and Interests," in Brieger, ed., *Medical America in the Nineteenth Century,* 67.
9. John Duffy makes the point that approximately 700 American physicians went to France to study from 1820 to 1860. See *The Healers,* 101. For other readings on American physicians in France, see Russell M. Jones, "American Doctors and the Parisian Medical World, 1830–1840," *Bulletin of the History of Medicine* 47 (1973): 40–65; and Irving A. Beck, "An Early American Journey Keyed to Medical Students: A Pioneer Contribution of Elisha Bartlett," *Bulletin of the History of Medicine* 40 (1966): 124–34.
10. See Katherine Bankole, *Slavery and Medicine: Enslavement and Medical Practices in Antebellum Louisiana* (New York: Garland, 1998), 134.
11. The goddess Ma'at was believed to represent the divine order of the universe at the inception of creation. A powerful goddess, Ma'at regulated the seasons, the stars' movement, and the relationship between men and gods. A temple at Karnak, Egypt, is dedicated to her memory. See Ian Shaw and Paul Nicholson, *British Museum Dictionary of Ancient Egypt* (London: British Museum Publications, 1995), 166.
12. Bankole, *Slavery and Medicine,* 134.
13. Bankole charts the eight concepts and corresponding components of the African Living Belief System in *Slavery and Medicine,* 134–35, Table 10.
14. Europeans and white Americans were suspicious of bathing (wetting the body all over). Many associated the advent of public bathhouses in the sixteenth century with the rise of syphilis, and, in the centuries that followed, many people preferred not to bathe. Slave healers saw the bath as a form of hygienic cleanliness. For a history of bathing, see Duffy, *The Healers,* 121.

15. Yarrow and lobelia were used to break fevers; red clover and hyssop, an aromatic mint, were used for teas; and nettle revived a numb or paralyzed limb. Nettle was also used for tea. It contained sulfur, potassium, iron, and calcium. See Shirley Boie, *Herb Teas for Health* (Los Angeles: Boie Enterprises, 1971), 197; and Wilbur H. Watson, ed., *Black Folk Medicine: The Therapeutic Significance of Faith and Trust* (New Brunswick, NJ: Transaction Books, 1984).
16. Janheinz Jahn, *Muntu: African Culture and the Western World*, trans. Marjorie Grene (New York: Grove Weidenfeld, 1989), 128.
17. In her discussion of survival tactics for those with few options, Janeway identifies bonding as a defense mechanism. See Elizabeth Janeway, *Powers of the Weak* (New York: Alfred A. Knopf, 1980), 172.
18. Nancy C. M. Hartsock, *Money, Sex and Power: Toward a Feminist Historical Materialism* (Boston: Northwestern UP, 1985), 125.
19. According to Wilbur H. Watson, Voodoo is a spiritual entity and a medical "system of beliefs about health and illness that facilitate coping with disorders of body and mind, as well as evil spirits." See Watson, *Black Folk Medicine*, 3. Expanding Watson's definition, Jean Price-Mars identifies Voodoo as a religion because "the initiated believe[s] in the existence of spiritual beings," because there exists "a hierarchical order of priests, a community of believers, temples, altars, ceremonies, and an oral tradition," and because a theology or conceptual system of beliefs defines the god's relationships to the universe and explains natural phenomena. See Jahn, *Muntu*, 32–33.
20. Variously referred to as Vodun, Vodu, Hoodoo, and Vadou, Voodoo in its original form was introduced into the United States at New Orleans via African slaves, coming either directly from Africa or brought into the country from Haiti. The most famous female Voodooist in New Orleans was Marie Laveau (1790–1881). Born a free quadroon, she was feared and praised for her magical powers by the residents of New Orleans. Her intuitiveness and influence in the city placed her in a position to collect pertinent information that she used as the foundation for her manipulations. She represented the retention of African religious beliefs expressed in Voodoo practices. See Virginia Gould, "Laveau, Marie," in Darlene Clark Hine, ed., *Black Women in America: An Historical Encyclopedia* (Brooklyn, NY: Carlson, 1993), I, 701.
21. Alexis Kagame cites two principles (Ntu and Nommo) and four basic categories (Muntu, Kintu, Hantu, and Kuntu) of African ontology. Jahn elucidates these principles and categories in *Muntu*, 96–155.
22. See Molefi K. Asante, *The Afrocentric Idea* (Philadelphia: Temple UP, 1987), 17.
23. Quoted in Jahn, *Muntu*, 133.
24. Celie's error violates the Arada rite practiced in Dahomey (now Benin), West Africa, birthplace of Voodoo (and namesake for which the priest Dahomey is a trope of). See chapter 2 of Jahn's *Muntu* for a brief discussion of the Arada rite.
25. Dr. Rush arrived at his theory after witnessing the loss of skin pigmentation on a slave named Henry Moss, who suffered from the hereditary disease that medical science now identifies as vitiligo. See Thomas Szasz, *The Manufacture of Madness: A Comparative Study of the Inquisition and the Mental Health Movement* (Syracuse: Syracuse UP, 1997), 154–55.
26. Benjamin Rush, "Observations Intended to Favor a Supposition That the Black Color (as It Is Called) of the Negroes Is Derived from the Leprosy," *Transactions of the American Philosophical Society* 4 (1799): 289. Rush's entire address to the American Philosophical Society on July 14, 1792, is reprinted in Louis Ruchames, ed., *Racial Thought in America*,

a Documentary History: From the Puritans to Abraham Lincoln (Amherst: U of Massachusetts P, 1969), 218–25.

27. Szasz, *The Manufacture of Madness,* 155.
28. Caroline Virginia Still Wiley Anderson (1848–1919), the daughter of Letitia and William Still, famed Underground Railroad founders in Philadelphia, attended Woman's Medical College in Philadelphia from 1876 to 1878. She was graduated from Woman's Medical College in 1878, three years after the graduation date for Beverly Jenkins's heroine. Nevertheless, Vivid's fictional representation of Anderson is a trope on the formally trained black women physicians who received degrees from America's respectable medical schools but were segregated into a limited practice.
29. The forerunner of Woman's Medical College, the Female Medical College of Pennsylvania was founded in 1850, and is considered the United States' first medical school for women. The medical school's early years were beset with difficulty, including its alleged association with Eclecticism from conservative male physicians and its closing in 1861. In 1862, it reopened as the Woman's Medical College of Pennsylvania; Ann Preston, its first graduate, became its director. It provided medical training for women of all races and nationalities and graduated several black women before 1900. These included (but are not limited to) Rebecca J. Cole (1867), the first black to receive a degree from that school; Caroline Still Wiley Anderson (1878), who started a private practice in Philadelphia and operated a dispensary and clinic at the Berea Presbyterian Church, where her husband preached; Matilda Arabella Evans (1897), who returned to her native South Carolina to begin a private practice in her home; and Lucy Hughes Brown (1894), who went back to North Carolina and established the Hospital and Nursing Training School for Negroes. Today, the Woman's Medical College building in Philadelphia survives as a haven for the elderly and the homeless. See Darlene Clark Hine, "Co-Laborers in the Work of the Lord"; Duffy, *The Healers,* 273; Margaret Hope Bacon, "Ann Preston: Pioneer Woman Doctor," *Friends Journal* (October 1999): 20–23.
30. The intersection of race and sex affected black women as well as white women who dared to seek a medical career. In 1850, male students at Harvard Medical School, for instance, protested the matriculation of Harriot Hunt, a middle-class Boston white woman, at the same time that they protested the admittance of three black males. The protesters gave similar reasons for denying the black men and Hunt. They charged that "socially repulsive" black men would devalue Harvard's diploma and that Hunt's admission would deflate "the dignity of the school." See Mary Roth Walsh, *"Doctors Wanted, No Women Need Apply": Sexual Barriers in the Medical Profession, 1835–1975* (New Haven: Yale UP, 1977), 32.
31. Richard Allen founded the Bethel African Methodist Episcopal Church in Philadelphia in 1794 to avoid racism in the white Methodist church he was attending. Yet, in his own church, Richard Allen discriminated against women trained to preach.
32. For specific and leading causes of deaths among infants for 1899–1900, see Table 1.1 in Samuel H. Preston and Michael R. Haines's *Fatal Years: Child Mortality in Late Nineteenth-Century America* (Princeton, NJ: Princeton UP, 1991), 4–5.
33. Department of Commerce, *Negro Population in the United States,* 315, Table 19.
34. In 1900, the collection of mortality statistics began the national death registration areas. Hypothetical life expectancy is computed at birth based on the average number of years a subject is expected to live, which in turn is based on the life expectancy chart heeded at birth. U.S. Bureau of the Census. *Historical Statistics of the United States: Colonial Times to 1970,* vol. 2 (Washington, DC: Government Printing Office, 1975), 55.

35. Duffy, *The Healers,* 95.
36. Ibid.
37. See Geoffrey Marks and William K. Beatty, *The Story of Medicine in America* (New York: Charles Scribner's, 1973), 174.
38. White men in the nineteenth and early twentieth centuries made public their damaging views about black women. James W. Jacks, in 1895, penned that black women had no virtue. See the introduction to this study. Another white man, a physician, in describing blacks' susceptibility to sexually transmitted diseases, wrote: "Virtue in the negro race is like angels' visits—few and far between. In a practice of sixteen years I have never examined a virgin negro over fourteen years of age." See Daniel David Quillian, "Racial Peculiarities: A Cause of the Prevalence of Syphilis in Negroes," *American Journal of Dermatology and Genito-Urinary Disfunction* 10 (July 1906): 277.

Chapter Four: Post-Reconstruction Activism: The Call to Be Educated and to Educate

1. Mary Smith Kelsey Peake (1823–1862), a Norfolk, Virginia, native, illegally taught slaves and free blacks in Hampton, Virginia, around 1851. She conducted day and night classes and was among the first colored teachers that the American Missionary Association supported. See Hine, *Black Women in America,* II, 914.
2. E. Belle Mitchell Jackson (1848–1942), a Danville, Kentucky, native was the first black teacher hired to educate African American soldiers at Camp Nelson, a union military facility in Kentucky, in 1865. At seventeen years of age, she showed remarkable strength when white missionary teachers at the camp refused to share eating and living quarters with her because of her race and petitioned the American Missionary Association for her dismissal. See Jessie Carney Smith, ed. *Notable Black Women* (Detroit: Gale Research, 1996), Book II, 317–18.
3. Anna Julia Cooper (1858–1964), born a slave in Raleigh, North Carolina, and educated at Oberlin College, held several teaching posts during post-Reconstruction. During her tenure at St. Augustine College in Raleigh, she chided state legislators for their failure to provide fair and equitable supplies to the colored youth at the institution. See Hine, *Black Women in America,* I, 276.
4. Fanny Jackson Coppin (1837–1913) was born a slave in Washington, D.C., and was educated at Oberlin College. Teacher and the first black female principal at the Institute for Colored Youth in Philadelphia, she started an Industrial Department to enable black youth at the school to meet employment demands in the trades. Hine, *Black Women in America,* I, 281–83.
5. Quoted in Belinda Hurmence, ed., *Before Freedom: 48 Oral Histories of Former North and South Carolina Slaves* (New York: Mentor, 1990), 16.
6. Robert C. Morris, *Reading, 'Riting, and Reconstruction: The Education of Freedmen in the South, 1861–1870* (Chicago: U of Chicago P, 1981), 85; Dorothy Sterling, ed., *We Are Your Sisters: Black Women in the Nineteenth Century* (New York: W. W. Norton, 1984), 377.
7. Darlene Clark Hine and Kathleen Thompson, eds., *A Shining Thread of Hope: The History of Black Women in America* (New York: Broadway Press, 1998), 160.

8. Edward H. Clarke, *Sex in Education; or, A Fair Chance for Girls* (Boston: James R. Osgood, 1874), 48.
9. Josephine J. Turpin, "Higher Education for Women," *The People's Advocate,* 12 April 1884: 1.
10. See Hine, *Black Women in America,* I, 383.
11. Calx, "Two Great Evils of Virginia and Their One Common Remedy," *Political Pamphlets* 41 (September 1859): 2, 5.
12. Henry Adams was also a political organizer. He could not always obtain financing for his followers, but he urged poor rural blacks in Louisiana and contiguous states to emigrate first to Liberia, and then to Kansas. See Nell Irvin Painter, *Black Exodusters: Black Migration to Kansas after Reconstruction* (New York: Alfred A. Knopf, 1977) 99–101.
13. Throughout the South, blacks followed those who urged them to resettle in Kansas. Black Kentuckians trailed behind William Smith and Thomas Harris, two black ministers from Tennessee who urged settlement in Nicodemus, Kansas. The largest number of blacks came from Mississippi, Louisiana, Tennessee, and Texas. They followed Benjamin "Pap" Singleton, a seventy-year-old, divinely inspired ex-slave who settled his followers in 1879 in the Singleton Colony, incorporated in Morris County, Kansas. See Norman L. Crockett, *The Black Towns* (Lawrence: Regents Press of Kansas, 1979), 2; and Nell Irvin Painter, *Black Exodusters: Black Migration to Kansas after Reconstruction,* 116.
14. Exodusters, or 'dusters, founded and settled in all-black towns in Kansas, which they referred to as Canaan. They compared themselves to the Old Testament Israelites who occupied the biblical Canaan, also known as Palestine and the Holy Land.
15. Henry Adams, *Senate Report 693,* U.S. Senate, 46th Congress, 2nd session, Report and Testimony of the Select Committee of the United States Senate to Investigate the Causes and Removal of the Negroes from the Southern States to the Northern States (Washington, DC: 1880), vol. 2, 184–85.
16. Robert G. Athearn, "Black Exodus: The Migration of 1879," *The Prairie Scout* 3 (1975): 93.
17. Painter, *Black Exodusters,* 257.
18. F. R. Guernsey, "The Negro Exodus," *The International Review* 7.4 (1879): 377.
19. John F. Slater, a Connecticut textile manufacturer, started the Slater Fund in 1882 when he donated one million dollars to Negro education. He specified that the money be used to uplift the emancipated slaves in the South and their children by conferring on them a Christian education. Slater's intent was to aid the economic advancement of blacks. See Roy E. Finkenbine, "'Our Little Circle': Benevolent Reformers, The Slater Fund, and the Argument for Black Industrial Education, 1882–1908." *Hayes Historical Journal* 6 (1986).
20. Anna T. Jeanes, a Quaker heiress, established the Rural School Fund in 1907, commonly known as the Jeanes Fund, to improve the quality of African American rural schools. Receiving financial support from the fund, many blacks became Jeanes teachers and improved the quality of rural black education. See Hine, *Black Women in America,* I, 632.
21. Marilyn Frye, "Oppression," in Paula S. Rothenberg, ed., *Race, Class, and Gender in the United States: An Integrated Study,* 2nd ed. (New York: St. Martin's P, 1992), 55.
22. For a fuller description of what "ladyhood" meant for white women, see Barbara Christian, *Black Feminist Criticism: Perspectives on Black Women Writers* (New York: Pergamon, 1985), 72.

23. Anna Julia Cooper, "The Higher Education of Women," in Charles Lemert and Esme Bahn, eds., *The Voice of Anna Julia Cooper: Including A Voice from the South and Other Important Essays, Papers, and Letters* (New York: Rowman and Littlefield, 1998), 78, 82.

Chapter Five: Early-Twentieth-Century Activism: Saving Land in Texas

1. The Land Loss Fund, "Working Together to Preserve African-American Land Ownership." Available at http://members.aol.com/tillery/llf.html. Accessed May 16, 2003.
2. See Loren Schweninger, *Black Property Owners in the South, 1790–1915* (Urbana: U of Illinois P, 1990), 86.
3. Ibid., 289, Table 34.
4. Mexia is located in the northeastern section of Limestone County and is approximately twelve miles northeast of Groesbeck. It is named in honor of Enrique Antonio Guillermo Mexia (1829–1896), son of José Antonio Mexia (1800–1839), the Mexican general who served under Santa Anna and whose family in 1833 purchased the 30-acre land grant. For a history of Limestone County, see Ray A. Walter, *History of Limestone County* (Austin: Von Boeckmann-Jones, 1959).
5. Nanine Simmons, "Best Early Mexia Oil Well Yielded 1,000 Barrels Hours," *Waco Times-Herald*, 9 Feb. 1955: 2.
6. Nanine Simmons, "Mexia's Population Once 55,000," *Waco Times-Herald*, 11 Feb. 1955: 10.
7. See Bunkley's afterword to *Black Gold* for more information on the oil boom in Mexia and its aftereffects.
8. Robert J. Art, "The Four Functions of Force," in Robert J. Art and Kenneth N. Waltz, eds., *The Use of Force: Military Power and International Politics* (New York: University Press of America, 1993), 4.
9. Dorothy Smith, *The Everyday World as Problematic: A Feminist Sociology* (Boston: Northeastern UP, 1987), 19–20.
10. Patricia Hill Collins, "The Social Construction of Black Feminist Thought," *Signs: Journal of Women in Culture and Society* 14 (Summer 1989): 761.

Bibliography

Adams, Henry. *Senate Report 693, II*. U.S. Senate, 46th Congress, 2nd session. Report and Testimony of the Select Committee of the United States Senate to Investigate the Causes and Removal of the Negroes from the Southern States to the Northern States, 3 vols. Washington, DC, 1880.

American Freedmen's Inquiry Commission, St. Louis, Mo., November-December 1863, RG 94, M 619, Roll 201 at 84. National Archives.

Art, Robert J., and Kenneth N. Waltz, eds. *The Use of Force: Military Power and International Politics*. New York: University Press of America, 1993.

Asante, Molefi K. *The Afrocentric Idea*. Philadelphia: Temple UP, 1987.

Athearn, Robert G. "Black Exodus: The Migration of 1879." *The Prairie Scout* 3 (1975): 86–97.

Bacon, Margaret Hope. "Ann Preston: Pioneer Woman Doctor." *Friends Journal* (October 1999): 20–23.

Bankole, Katherine. *Slavery and Medicine: Enslavement and Medical Practices in Antebellum Louisiana*. New York: Garland, 1998.

Bardaglio, Peter. "The Children of Jubilee: African American Childhood in Wartime." *Divided Houses: Gender and the Civil War*. Ed. Catherine Clinton and Nina Silber. New York: Oxford UP, 1992. 213–29.

Bass, Feris A., and B. R. Brunson, eds. *Fragile Empires: The Texas Correspondence of Samuel Swartwout and James Morgan, 1836–1856*. Austin: Shoal Creek, 1978.

Beck, Irving A. "An Early American Journey Keyed to Medical Students: A Pioneer Contribution of Elisha Bartlett." *Bulletin of the History of Medicine* 40 (1966): 124–34.

Begeman, June A. "Lynchburg, Cedar Bayou and Morgan's Point Ferryboats: Historical Highlights." *Touchstone* 7 (1988): 9–17.

Bibb, Henry. "The Narrative of Henry Bibb." 1817. In *Puttin' on Ole Massa: The Slave Narratives of Henry Bibb, William Wells Brown, and Solomon Northup.* Ed. Gilbert Osofsky. New York: Harper and Row, 1969. 64–171.

Boie, Shirley. *Herb Teas for Health.* Los Angeles: Boie Enterprises, 1971.

Brieger, Gert H., ed. *Medical America in the Nineteenth Century: Readings from the Literature.* Baltimore: Johns Hopkins P, 1972.

Brooks, Peter. *Reading for the Plot: Design and Intention in Narrative.* New York: Alfred A. Knopf, 1984.

Brown, William Wells. *Clotel; or, The President's Daughter. A Narrative of Slave Life in the United States.* 1853. New York: Collier Books, 1970.

Brunson, B. R., and Andrew Forest Muir. "Morgan, James." *Handbook of Texas Online*, at http://www.tsha.utexas.edu/handbook/online/articles/view/MM/fm050.html. Accessed 14 May 2003.

Buckmaster, Henrietta. *Let My People Go: The Story of the Underground Railroad and the Growth of the Abolitionist Movement.* 1941. Columbia: U of South Carolina P, 1993.

Bunkley, Anita Richmond. *Black Gold.* New York: Signet, 1995.

———. *Emily, the Yellow Rose: A Texas Legend.* Houston: Rinard, 1989.

Calx, "Two Great Evils of Virginia and Their One Common Remedy." *Political Pamphlets* 41 (September 1859): 1–18.

Campbell, Randolph B. *An Empire for Slavery: The Peculiar Institution in Texas: 1821–1865.* Baton Rouge: Louisiana State UP, 1989.

Carroll, Bernice. "Peace Research: The Cult of Power." *Journal of Conflict Resolution* 16.4 (1972): 585–616.

Christian, Barbara. *Black Feminist Criticism: Perspectives on Black Women Writers.* New York: Pergamon, 1985.

———. *Black Women Novelists: The Development of a Tradition, 1892–1976.* Westport, CT: Greenwood, 1980.

Clarke, Edward H. *Sex in Education; or, A Fair Chance for Girls.* Boston: James R. Osgood, 1874.

Collins, Patricia Hill. *Black Feminist Thought: Knowledge, Consciousness, and the Politics of Empowerment.* New York: Routledge, 1991.

———. "The Social Construction of Black Feminist Thought." *Signs: Journal of Women in Culture and Society* 14 (Summer 1989): 745–73.

Cooper, Anna Julia. "The Higher Education of Women." *The Voice of Anna Julia Cooper: Including A Voice from the South and Other Important Essays, Papers, and Letters.* Ed. Charles Lemert and Esme Bahn. New York: Rowan and Littlefield, 1998. 72–87.

———. *A Voice from the South.* 1892. New York: Oxford UP, 1988.

Craft, Francine. *The Black Pearl.* New York: Kensington, 1996.

Crockett, Norman L. *The Black Towns.* Lawrence: Regent Press of Kansas, 1979.

Cullen-Dupont, Katheryn, ed. "Phyllis Schafly." *American Women Activists' Writings: An Anthology, 1637–2002.* New York: Cooper Square P, 2002. 509–16.

Davis, Elizabeth Lindsay. *Lifting as They Climb: African American Women Writers, 1910–1940.* New York: G. K. Hall, 1995.

Decker, Ed. "Beverly Jenkins." *Contemporary Black Biography.* Eds. Mpho L. Mabunda and Shirelle Phelps. Vol. 14. Detroit: Gale Research, 1997: 138–40.

Dekker, George. *The American Historical Romance*. Cambridge and New York: Cambridge UP, 1987.

de Lauretis, Teresa. *Technologies of Gender: Essays on Theory, Film, and Fiction*. Bloomington: Indiana UP, 1987.

Department of Commerce, Bureau of the Census. *Negro Population in the United States, 1790–1915*. 1918. New York: Arno Press, 1968.

Dormon, James H., ed. *Creoles of Color of the Gulf South*. Knoxville: U of Tennessee P, 1996.

Du Bois, W. E. B. *Dark Princess: A Romance*. New York: Harcourt, Brace, 1928.

Duffy, John. *The Healers: A History of American Medicine*. Urbana: U of Illinois P, 1979.

Fabi, M. Giulia. *Passing and the Rise of the African American Novel*. Urbana: U of Illinois P, 2001.

Finkenbine, Roy E. "'Our Little Circle': Benevolent Reformers, The Slater Fund, and the Argument for Black Industrial Education, 1882–1908." *Hayes Historical Journal* 6 (1986): 6–22.

Franke, Katherine M. "Taking Care." *Chicago-Kent Law Review* 76 (2001): 1541–55.

Frye, Marilyn. "Oppression." *Race, Class, and Gender in the United States: An Integrated Study*, 2nd ed. Ed. Paula S. Rothenberg. New York: St. Martin's Press, 1992. 54–57.

Gandy, Moses. *Narrative of the Life of Moses Gandy, Late a Slave*. Boston: Oliver Johnson, 1844.

Gayle, Roberta. *Moonrise*. New York: Pinnacle, 1996.

———. *Sunshine and Shadows*. New York: Kensington, 1995.

Genovese, Eugene D. *Roll, Jordan Roll: The World the Slaves Made*. New York: Pantheon, 1974.

Goodson, Marita Graham. "Medical-Botanical Contributions of African Slave Women to American Medicine." *Black Women in United States History*. Ed. Darlene Clark Hine. 2 vols. Brooklyn, NY: Carlson Press, 1990. II, 473–84.

Guernsey, F. R. "The Negro Exodus." *The International Review* 7.4 (1879): 373–90.

Gunn, Gay G. *Nowhere to Run*. Columbus, MS: Genesis P, 1997.

Gutman, Herbert George. *The Black Family in Slavery and Freedom, 1750–1925*. New York: Pantheon, 1976.

Hailstock, Shirley. *Clara's Promise*. New York: Windsor, 1995.

Harley, Sharon, and Rosalyn Terborg-Penn, eds. *The Afro-American Woman: Struggles and Images*. Baltimore: Black Classic P, 1978.

Harper, Frances W. *Iola Leroy, or Shadows Uplifted*. 1892. New York: AMS, 1971.

———. Minnie's Sacrifice, Sowing and Reaping, *and* Trial and Triumph*: Three Rediscovered Novels*. Ed. Frances Smith Foster. Boston: Beacon, 1994.

Harrigan, Stephen. "The Yellow Rose of Texas." *Texas Monthly* 12 (April 1984).

Hartsock, Nancy C. M. *Money, Sex and Power: Toward a Feminist Historical Materialism*. Boston: Northwestern UP, 1983.

Henson, Margaret Swett. "She's the Real Thing," *Texas Highways* 33.4 (April 1986): 60–61.

Higginbotham, Evelyn. "African American Women's History and the Metalanguage of Race." *Signs: Journal of Women in Culture and Society* 17 (Winter 1992): 251–74.

Hine, Darlene Clark, ed. *Black Women in America: An Historical Encyclopedia*. 2 Vols. New York: Carlson, 1993.

———. "Co-Laborers in the Work of the Lord: Nineteenth-Century Black Women Physicians." *Black Women in United States History*. Ed. Hine. 2 vols. Brooklyn, NY: Carlson Press, 1990. II, 637–52.

Hine, Darlene Clark, and Kathleen Thompson, eds. *A Shining Thread of Hope: The History of Black Women in America*. New York: Broadway Press, 1998.

hooks, bell. *Sisters of the Yam: Black Women and Self-Discovery*. Boston: South End, 1993.

Hopkins, Pauline. *Contending Forces: A Romance Illustrative of Negro Life in the South*. 1900. New York: AMS, 1971.

Horton, James Oliver. *Free People of Color: Inside the African American Community*. Washington, DC: Smithsonian Institution P, 1993.

Hudson-Weems, Clenora. *African Womanism: Reclaiming Ourselves*. Troy, MI: Bedford, 1993.

Hurmence, Belinda, ed. *Before Freedom: 48 Oral Histories of Former North and South Carolina Slaves*. Winston Salem, NC: John F. Blair Publisher, 1990.

Hurston, Zora Neale. *Their Eyes Were Watching God*. Philadelphia: J. B. Lippincott, 1937.

Irigaray, Luce. *This Sex Which Is Not One*. Trans. from French by Catherine Porter and Carolyn Burke. Ithaca: Cornell UP, 1985.

Irons, Glenwood, ed. *Gender, Language and Myth: Essays on Popular Narrative*. Toronto and Buffalo: U of Toronto P, 1992.

Jahn, Janheinz. *Muntu: African Culture and the Western World*. Trans. Marjorie Grene. New York: Grove: Weidenfeld, 1989.

Janeway, Elizabeth. *Powers of the Weak*. New York: Alfred A. Knopf, 1980.

Jefferson, Thomas. *Notes on the State of Virginia*. Ed. William Peden. Chapel Hill: U of North Carolina P, 1955.

Jenkins, Beverly. *Indigo*. New York: Avon, 1996.

———. *Night Song*. New York: Avon, 1994.

———. *Through the Storm*. New York: Avon, 1998.

———. *Vivid*. New York: Avon, 1995.

Jones, Jacqueline. *Labor of Love, Labor of Sorrow: Black Women, Work, and the Family from Slavery to the Present*. New York: Basic Books, 1985.

Jones, Russell M. "American Doctors and the Parisian Medical World, 1830–1840." *Bulletin of the History of Medicine* 47 (1973): 40–65.

Jordan, Winthrop D. *White over Black: American Attitudes toward the Negro, 1550–1812*. New York: Norton, 1977.

Kagame, Alexis. *La Philosophie Bantu-Rwandaise de l'Être*. Bruxelles, 1951.

The Land Loss Fund. "Working Together to Preserve African-American Landownership." Online at http://members.aol.com/tillery/llf.html. Accessed 16 May 2003.

Lee, Jarena. "The Life and Religious Experiences of Jarena Lee: A Colored Lady Giving an Account of Her Call to Preach the Gospel." *Early Negro Writing, 1760–1837*. Ed. Dorothy Porter. Boston: Beacon, 1971.

Loewenberg, Bert, and Ruth Bogin. *Black Women in Nineteenth-Century American Life: Their Works, Their Thoughts, Their Feelings*. University Park: Pennsylvania State UP, 1976.

Lundy, Benjamin. *The Life, Travels and Opinions of Benjamin Lundy, Including His Journeys to Texas and Mexico; with a Sketch of Contemporary Events, and a Notice of the Revolution of Hayti*. 1847. New York: Negro Universities P, 1969.

"'Mammy' Pleasant: Memoirs and Autobiography." *The Pandex of the Press* 1 (January 1902), 1–6.

Marks, Geoffrey, and William K. Beatty. *The Story of Medicine in America.* New York: Scribner, 1973.

Martin, Elmer P., and Joanne Mitchell Martin. *Social Work and the Black Experience.* Washington, DC: National Association of Social Workers, 1995.

Martin, Wallace. *Recent Theories of Narrative.* Ithaca, NY: Cornell UP, 1986.

McMillan, Terry. *Disappearing Acts.* New York: Washington Square, 1989.

Morris, Robert C. *Reading, 'Riting, and Reconstruction: The Education of Freedmen in the South, 1861–1870.* Chicago: U of Chicago P, 1981.

Naylor, Gloria. *Mama Day.* New York: Vintage, 1988.

Noble, Jeanne L. *Beautiful, Also, Are the Souls of My Black Sisters: A History of the Black Woman in America.* Englewood Cliffs, NJ: Prentice-Hall, 1978.

Office of Assistant Commissioner, Bureau of Refugees, Freedmen and Abandoned Lands, Circular No. 4, Vicksburg, MS. (July 29, 1865), RG 826, Roll 28, frame 259, National Archives.

Ore, Tracy E., ed. *The Social Construction of Difference and Inequality: Race, Class, Gender, and Sexuality.* Mountain View, CA: Mayfield, 2000.

Painter, Nell Irvin. *Exodusters: Black Migration to Kansas after Reconstruction.* New York: Alfred A. Knopf, 1977.

Parham, Thomas A., Joseph L. White, and Adisa Ajamu. *The Psychology of Blacks: An African-Centered Perspective.* Upper Saddle River, NJ: Prentice Hall, 1999.

Parrish, Anne. *A Clouded Star.* New York: Harper, 1948.

Pettit, Florence Harvey. *America's Indigo Blues: Resist-printed and Dyed Textiles of the Eighteenth Century.* New York: Hastings House, 1974.

Porcher, Francis Peyre. *A Medico-Botanical Catalogue of the Plants and Ferns of St. John's Berkeley, South Carolina.* Thesis. Charles Medical School, Charleston, 1847.

———. *Resources of the Southern Fields and Forests, Medical, Economical, and Agricultural. Being Also a Medical Botany of the Confederate States; with Practical Information on the Useful Properties of the Trees, Plants and Shrubs . . . Prepared and Published by Order of the Surgeon-general* [of the Confederate States of America], *Richmond, Va.* Charleston: Steam-Power Press of Evans and Cogswell, 1863.

Preston, Samuel H., and Michael R. Haines. *Fatal Years: Child Mortality in Late Nineteenth-Century America.* Princeton, NJ: Princeton UP, 1991.

Quarles, Benjamin. *Black Abolitionists.* New York: Oxford UP, 1969.

———. *The Negro in the Making of America.* New York: Collier, 1969.

Quillian, Daniel David. "Racial Peculiarities: A Cause of the Prevalence of Syphilis in Negroes." *American Journal of Dermatology and Genito-Urinary Disfunction* 10 (July 1906).

Ray, Francis. *The Bargain.* New York: Pinnacle, 1995.

Reiser, Christa. *Reflections on Anger: Women and Men in a Changing Society.* Westport, CT: Praeger, 1999.

Ricoeur, Paul. *Time and Narrative.* Trans. from the French by Kathleen McLaughlin and David Pellauer. 3 vols. Chicago: U of Chicago P, 1984.

Riley, Mildred. *Midnight Moon.* New York: Pinnacle, 1995.

Ripley, C. Peter. *Slaves and Freedmen in Civil War Louisiana*. Baton Rouge: Louisiana State UP, 1976.

Ruchames, Louis, ed. *Racial Thought in America, a Documentary History: From the Puritans to Abraham Lincoln*. Amherst: U of Massachusetts P, 1969.

Rush, Benjamin. "Observations Intended to Favor a Supposition That the Black Color (as It Is Called) of the Negroes Is Derived from the Leprosy." *Transactions* 4 (1799): 289–97.

"San Felipe de Austin, Texas." *Handbook of Texas Online*. http://www.tsha.utexas.edu/handbook/online/articles/view/SS/hls10.html. Accessed 14 May 2003.

Schoen, Harold. "The Free Negro in the Republic of Texas: Legal Status." *Southwestern Quarterly* 39 (April 1936): 292–308.

Schweninger, Loren. *Black Property Owners of the South, 1790–1915*. Urbana: U of Illinois P, 1990.

Shaw, Ian, and Paul Nicholson. *British Museum Dictionary of Ancient Egypt*. London: British Museum Publications Ltd., 1995.

Simmons, Nanine. "Best Early Mexia Oil Well Yielded 1,000 Barrel Hours." *Waco Times-Herald*, 9 Feb 1955: 1–2.

———. "Mexia's Population Once 55,000." *Waco Times-Herald*, 11 Feb 1955: 10.

Smith, Barbara. "Toward a Black Feminist Criticism." *But Some of Us Are Brave*. Ed. Gloria T. Hull, Patricia Bell Scott, and Barbara Smith, Old Westbury, NY: Feminist P, 1982. 157–75.

Smith, Dorothy. *The Everyday World as Problematic: A Feminist Sociology*. Boston: Northeastern UP, 1987.

Smith, Jessie Carney, ed. *Notable Black American Women*. Book II. Detroit: Gale Research, 1996.

Sterling, Dorothy, ed., *We Are Your Sisters: Black Women in the Nineteenth Century*. New York: W. W. Norton, 1984.

Stevenson, Brenda E. *Life in Black and White: Family and Community in the Slave South*. New York: Oxford UP, 1996.

Stewart, F. Campbell. "The Actual Condition of the Medical Profession in This Country; with a Brief Account of Some of the Causes Which Tend to Impede Its Progress and Interfere with Its Honors and Interests." *Medical America in the Nineteenth-Century: Readings from the Literature*. Ed. Gert H. Brieger. Baltimore: Johns Hopkins P, 1972. 63–74.

Stewart, Maria. *Maria W. Stewart: America's First Black Woman Political Writer: Essays and Speeches*. Ed. Marilyn Richardson. Bloomington and Indianapolis: Indiana UP, 1987.

Szasz, Thomas. *The Manufacture of Madness: A Comparative Study of the Inquisition and the Mental Health Movement*. Syracuse: Syracuse UP, 1997.

Tate, Claudia. *Black Women Writers at Work*. New York: Continuum, 1983.

———. *Domestic Allegories of Political Desire: The Black Heroine's Text at the Turn of the Century*. New York: Oxford UP, 1992.

Templeton, John William. *Our Roots Run Deep: The Black Experience in California*. 4 vols. San Jose, CA: Electron Access Inc., 1997.

Thurman, Sue Bailey. *Pioneers of Negro Origin in California*. San Francisco: Acme, 1952.

Townsend, J. "Francis Peyre Porcher." *Annals of Medical History*. Third Series, I (1939): 177–88.

Turner, Martha Anne. *The Yellow Rose of Texas: Her Saga and Her Song, with the Santa Anna Legend*. Austin: Shoal Creek Publishers, 1976.

Turpin, Josephine J. "Higher Education for Women." *The People's Advocate,* 12 April 1884: 1.

U.S. Bureau of the Census. *Historical Statistics of the United States: Colonial Times to 1970.* 2 vols. Washington, DC: Government Printing Office, 1975.

Vaughn, Patricia. *Murmur of Rain.* New York: Pocket Books, 1996.

———. *Shadows on the Bayou.* New York: Pocket Books, 1998.

Walker, David. *Walker's Appeal, in Four Articles; Together with a Preamble, to the Coloured Citizens of the World, but in Particular, and Very Expressly, to Those of the United States of America, Written in Boston, State of Massachusetts, September 28, 1829.* Available at http://docsouth.unc.edu/nc/walker/walker.html. Accessed 13 May 2003.

Walker, Margaret. *Jubilee.* Boston: Houghton Mifflin, 1966.

Walsh, Mary Roth. *"Doctors Wanted: No Woman Need Apply": Sexual Barriers in the Medical Profession, 1835–1975.* New York: Yale UP, 1977.

Walter, Ray A. *History of Limestone County.* Austin: Von Boeckmann-Jones, 1959.

"Washington." *Texas Online.* At http://www.texas-on-line.com/graphic/washngtn.htm. Accessed 20 April 2001.

Watson, Wilbur H., ed. *Black Folk Medicine: The Therapeutic Significance of Faith and Trust.* New Brunswick, NJ: Transaction Books, 1984.

Wharton, Clarence Ray. *Wharton's History of Fort Bend County.* San Antonio: The Naylor Co., 1939.

Williams, David A. *Bricks without Straw: A Comprehensive History of African Americans in Texas.* Austin: Eakin, 1997.

Wright, Sarah E. *This Child's Gonna Live.* New York: Delacorte, 1969.

Yaeger, Patricia. *Honey-Mad Women: Emancipatory Strategies in Women's Writings.* New York: Columbia UP, 1988.

Yerby, Frank. *The Foxes of Harrow.* New York: Dial, 1946.

Index

-C-

-D-

-E-

-F-

-G-

-H-

-I-

-J-

-K-

-L-

-M-

-N-

-O-

-P-

-Q-

-R-

-S-

-T-

-V-

-W-

-Y-

AFRICAN AMERICAN LITERATURE AND CULTURE

EXPANDING AND EXPLODING THE BOUNDARIES

General Editor
Carlyle V. Thompson

The purpose of this series is to present innovative, in-depth, and provocatively critical literary and cultural investigations of critical issues in African American literature and life. We welcome critiques of fiction, poetry, drama, film, sports, and popular culture. Of particular interest are literary and cultural analyses that involve contemporary psychoanalytical criticism, new historicism, deconstructionism, critical race theory, critical legal theory, and critical gender theory.

For additional information about this series or for the submission of manuscripts, please contact:

Peter Lang Publishing, Inc.
Acquisitions Department
275 Seventh Avenue, 28th floor
New York, New York 10001

To order other books in this series, please contact our Customer Service Department:

(800) 770-LANG (within the U.S.)
(212) 647-7706 (outside the U.S.)
(212) 647-7707 FAX

Or browse online by series:

www.peterlangusa.com